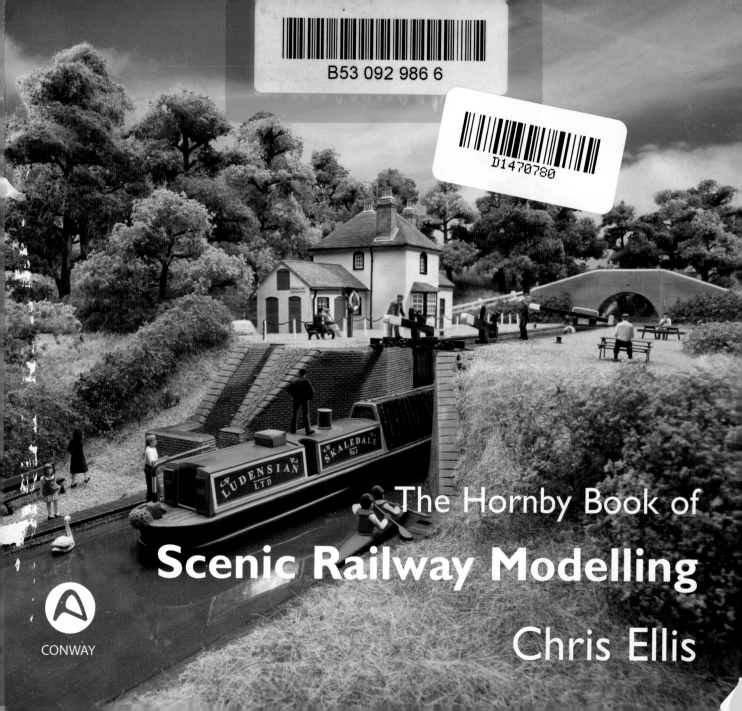

The Hornby Book of
Scenic Railway Modelling

Chris Ellis

CONWAY

A Conway Book

All photography © Chris Ellis,
© Hornby® Plc. © Mark Warrick page
80/81, Jeff Dalton pages 88/89, 116
and 144/145
Text © Navigator Guides Ltd 2010

This edition published in 2010 by
Conway
An imprint of Anova Books Group
10 Southcombe Street
London
W14 0RA

British Library Cataloguing in
Publication Data:
A catalogue record for this book is
available from the British Library.

ISBN 978 1 84486 112 5

Distributed in the U.S. and Canada
by: Sterling Publishing Co., Inc.
387 Park Avenue South
New York, NY 10016-8810

Designed and produced by Navigator
Guides www.navigatorguides.com
Printed and bound by Times Offset
Sdn Bhd, Malaysia

Acknowledgements
Hornby® would like to thank DSP
Ltd, Tunbridge Wells, Kent and
Thomas Neile Digital Photography,
Whitstable, Kent.

The publishers would like to thank
the cooperation of Hornby plc in
the making of this book. Use of the
Hornby Trade Mark by kind
permission of Hornby Hobbies Ltd.

Contents

Introduction

Once you have completed your baseboard, which was covered in the companion book The Hornby Book of Model Railways, the really absorbing part of the hobby is completing the 'world in miniature'. This involves giving it a realistic setting and convincing ambiance. Real railways run through cities, towns, and countryside, and depending on their location – which you may determine by your choice of period and setting – they may serve industry, harbours and tourist areas, or run through mountainous areas, lowlands or coastal plains to mention just a few examples. Modelling the scenery to depict your chosen setting is both creative and challenging.

If you are one of the many readers of this book who has been to a local model railway show or exhibition, where a number of working layouts are on display, you will most certainly have been impressed by some layouts more than others. If you think back, it was probably the realism that most caught your imagination. Convincing looking model trains running through very realistic miniature settings would certainly have caught your eye more readily than layouts where the scenery was crude or scanty or where there was hardly any scenery at all.

This book starts with some very simple ideas for those starting out with their first train sets, an area seldom covered in other books on scenic modelling. It then goes on to cover the conventional idea of scenic development in all its aspects, with some modern methods too, and some very simple and mostly inexpensive ones. You can pick and choose from the techniques and material covererd here, but the great advantage of scenic modelling is that you can always return to the layout and try again and as

The author with James May at his *Toy Stories* Toy Fair

your skill develops over the years you can replace earlier work. It is often said that a model railway layout is never finished and in the case of of ever-improving scenic skills this is very true. This book should give you plenty of ideas to keep you busy.

As ever there are a number of friends and colleagues to thank for their assistance with the preparation of this book, especially Brenda Sherwood for setting the manuscript, Jack Trollope for most of the diagrams and plans, Simon Kohler at Hornby for help and permission to use some Hornby illustrations, Sean Domeny for provision of the main Hornby photographs, and Nevile Reid who made some of the scenic settings illustrated. Jack Chipperfield, Andrew Knights, Ian Dack, Richard Gardner, and others mentioned by name in the text, supplied ideas or illustrations used in the book.

Chris Ellis 2010

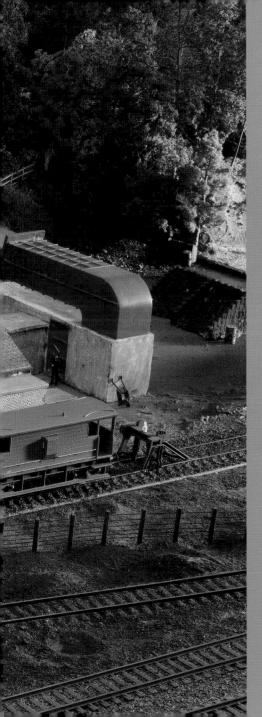

Chapter One

Scenic planning

Getting started

You may think that the ability to make the landscape, add the surface details, depict rivers, and so on, is all you need to succeed with scenic work. But it is rather more complex than that, at least if you are going to get the best out of a project. Most aspects of model railways overlap, even if they are dealt with separately. Thus you need to have the track laid properly and trains running efficiently before you start the scenic work. This avoids the problem of having a charming scenic setting but locomotives that have to be pushed to stop them stalling and coaches that derail on every curve. It seems obvious, but I've seen it happen often enough.

The other matter that figures large in proceedings is your choice of layout and layout subject. Some are happy enough with a nondescript setting and rather random scenic surrounds of hills and trees, etc, but once you are familiar with the hobby's potential, and the huge choice of models you may get slightly more ambitious ideas. First of all, most enthusiasts have favourite companies or eras, frequently linked to nostalgic memories, and this must be squared with the space available for a layout. Lucky modellers with a large spare room available will have few space limitations, but very many people live in small houses or apartments where space is at a premium. You may only have room for a shelf type layout, or an L-shaped layout in a corner. You may even have to make do with a portable layout that is stowed away when not in use.

So you need to choose a layout that fits the space available and work out a theme or subject for the setting. This in turn will affect the scenic development. But if you do only have space for a small layout there is no need to feel disadvantaged, not least because there will be less to do in both construction and scenic work, which can have advantages of its own in the way of cost and time.

There are published layout plans in abundance, appearing in track plan books, some model railway books, and the model railway magazines. Sometimes these have some scenic suggestions, but often they don't. There's no problem finding a plan you like, but before rushing into building it, spend some time doing the scenic planning which will give you an idea of what you need in the way of scenic materials and structures.

To see a practical example take a look at the layout plan printed on page 9. As it happens this is a very famous layout indeed, probably the first ever scale OO/HO layout with 2-rail DC power, built by model railway pioneer A.R. Walkley in 1925, but as effective today as it was when first built. In fact quite a lot of modellers over the years have made versions of it, sometimes with slight variations. Being essentially a goods yard it has a lot of operating possibilities for a small locomotive and 6-8 wagons. Mr Walkley also developed an automatic coupler that worked on the same principle as today's standard tension-lock type used by Hornby and others.

However, we are concerned with the scenic work. Jack Trollope has drawn out the plan for modern Hornby track and indicated all the features that Mr Walkley had on the layout. You can do this on any other track plan that lacks any scenic indications. Draw it out roughly to scale and pencil in the features you desire. On the Walkley Goods Yard layout, note the hill and tunnel at the left end where the line passes along, in theory, to the rest of the rail system. It would also allow extension on to another baseboard later if more space becomes available. Along the back of this layout is a backscene, country in character, so you will need suitable backscenes (several are available) to 6ft (180cm) in length.

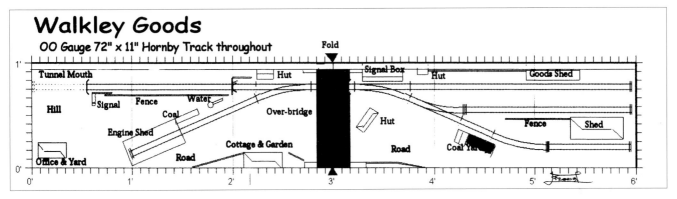

Figure 1.1 Track plan for Walkley Goods Yard, a classic small OO/HO layout project for a space 6ft (180cm) x 11in (28cm), with all structures and scenic features indicated.

Clearly you'll need a tunnel mouth, an engine shed, coal stage, water crane, fencing, two yard offices, a low relief goods shed, a larger shed or warehouse, coal staithes, a small signal box, two huts, and a cottage. A removable road bridge across the centre of the layout was a feature of the original layout which folded in the middle for portability, but the bridge could be optional, and you could make the layout a rigid 6ft long if you have the room.

With all the features listed you know which structures you'll need to buy or build (not necessarily all at once - get them as work proceeds). Most of the structures are in the Skaledale range as it happens (eg, R8972 Miner's Cottages would be ideal for the cottage marked), but kits or scratch-built structures could be used as well. Clearly you

have to build a hill, a road, and the yard area, all using the techniques described later. This all gives a good idea of the project ahead - what I like to call 'scenic planning'.

But it does not quite end there. Mr Walkley lived near the SR main line from Waterloo so he gave his layout a distinctly Southern Railway setting when it came to the backscene and scenic work. He built a SR M7 0-4-4T for the layout, too, but if you follow his inspiration today there is a superb M7 in several versions in the Hornby range. However, if you used this layout plan you could follow your own fancy. For example a GWR enthusiast might want to use a pannier tank engine and GWR Toad brake van, a 'West Country' backscene, and stone-finished buildings rather than the red brick ones Mr

Walkley used. Further variations are possible, such as BR diesel era with the fine Hornby 08 diesel shunter as the locomotive and mostly BR standard wagons. This suggests a possible variation in that the steam age engine shed could be replaced with an oil depot or timber yard to generate even more shunting. For the BR 'blue' period the yard office might even be a modern portable cabin as in the Skaledale range (R8757) and the coal staithes might be replaced by a crane, provender store, or freight platform.

From this you'll see that even a small layout has big but satisfying potential, and the scenic development is integral with all other considerations. Any other small layout can be projected as an exercise on paper like this to see how you can expect it to work out.

Figure 1.2 Julian Andrews built this small layout as an imagined branch of the Weston, Clevedon and Portishead Light Railway. Simple scratch-built store shed and mill form the background and the goods yard is realistically textured.

Figure 1.3 General view of the station on Richard Gardner's large OO gauge Stokenham layout, here running in BR(W) mode, though it can also run in GWR mode with period locomotives.

Later in this book you'll see two small layouts in industrial settings where the entire scenic development consists only of large workshop or manufacturing structures with no 'countryside' at all, and these are an opposite contrast to the open country nature of the Walkley Goods Yard.

Moving on

There is even more scenic planning needed if you have more ambitious layout ideas. One popular concept is to build a 'might have been' railway set in an actual location to give a good idea of how the real thing might have looked if it had ever been built. Richard Gardner built a superb 'might have been' OO gauge layout, Stokenham, which has been seen at a lot of model shows over the years. The GWR never built a route across the South Hams area of Devon, but Richard did an actual survey of the area, by way of maps and visits and built the sort of station at Stokenham that the GWR would have probably built had they followed that route. Richard Gardner is a talented artist, and from photographs he painted a backscene of the actual Stokenham area as it would be seen from the train, complete with the prominent church. It is so convincing that some people who saw the layout thought the GWR really had run through Stokenham.

Another enthusiast, Ian Dack, did a similar exercise to create the Midland and Great Northern Joint Railway Blakeney branch in north Norfolk. This had been proposed, but never built, so Ian built it in miniature, again after studying the maps, the proposed route, and a lot of photographs to get the scenic setting right. Because he lived near the area he was, too, familiar with the styles of building and the way the land and vegetation looked in those parts. More recently Ian has done a highly detailed survey of the Wells Quay Tramway which ran through the streets on to the quayside at Wells-next-the-Sea in Norfolk to enable this actual fascinating little line to be built in miniature.

Even if you are restricted to small layouts, the 'might have been' theme can be used. One layout I built in the 1980s featured the proposed, but never completed, extension of the Dyserth branch in north Wales on to Felindre. Part of the track bed for the extension was actually built but the real project was never completed. My small (5ft long) layout imagined what the new terminus at Felindre might have looked like. More recently I did a similar exercise for Welney, an extension once

Figure 1.4 Brian Taylor's OO gauge Snailspeed Light Railway is entirely freelance, but captures well the charm of a country town in southern England. Only the foreground buildings and those behind the van are fully modelled. The rest of the town is on the hand painted backscene.

Figure 1.5 The small ground level station Weston Road on the Weston, Clevedon, and Portishead Light Railway OO gauge layout of Julian Andrews. Only the station and trees are fully modelled.

Figure 1.6 You can get good ideas from other layouts seen at model shows. This canal basin and wharf on the Grand Junction Canal is modelled on the Wag's Wharf layout of Geoff Evans, a large scale (16mm to 1ft) model, and could be done equally well in 4mm scale using Skaledale canal boats and a small overhead crane.

set in Canada, USA, France, Germany and other countries, done by British modellers and all very convincing. Obviously, there is no reason why you should not model an actual location, and this has been done quite often with, for example, the GWR Ashburton and Hemyock branches. It is not too common, however, because real settings tend to stretch over a longer area than you might think and usually demand a lot of space. With a 'might have been' or entirely freelance layout you can control the length to suit your available space.

Research

Common to all layout projects is that the scenics and settings will demand the appropriate treatment to look convincing - rolling downland and woods for Sussex, perhaps, mountains and rocky outcrops for a Scottish Highland setting, flat fenlands for East Anglia and so forth. Which is why 'scenic planning' is necessary.

Unless you live near your projected layout's location, you will need to do some research to get a good idea of the 'look' of a setting. Books, Ordnance Survey maps, and videos/DVDs are all useful for this particularly if you've never been near the area involved. Once I built a layout set on the

proposed for the famous Wisbech and Upwell Tramway. This was never actually built, but I built an imagined one in Wisbech and Upwell Tramway complete with structures of typical local character, and flat terrain with wide river.

Examples of this sort of thing are endless: imagined extensions to the Wantage Tramway have been built quite frequently, as have extensions or imagined additions in all sorts of favourite locations such as Cornwall or the Scottish Highlands. There is almost no limit to this approach. The same can be done for overseas railways, and I've come across 'might have been' layouts northern tip of Rugen Island off the German Baltic coast. I've never been there, but with a guide book of the area and a borrowed travel video it came out well enough for someone who was familiar with the place to recognise the layout setting! It didn't end with the scenery alone, for I also modelled a couple of the distinctive type of fishing boats, again taken from guide book photographs.

Finally it is always a good idea to keep the future in mind. I've got a cuttings book and in it I put any pictures and articles of interesting places, settings, and areas that could possibly offer ideas for layouts I might build one day. Travel supplements in newspapers are a good source of these, as are holiday brochures and visitor leaflets.

Figure 1.7 Superb factory and warehouse modelling on the big Dewsbury Midland layout of Manchester Model Railway Society. This is a 'might have been' setting at Dewsbury based on an actual project, incorporating mostly city modelling as well with many buildings based on real originals and entirely scratch-built.

Figure 1.8 Andrew Knights built a small 7ft x 1ft 00 gauge layout based on a small goods yard that once ran alongside the Alderman canal in Ipswich, Suffolk. This is the coal depot at the end of the line.

Chapter Two

Before you begin

While scenic planning in the way suggested in the previous chapter will help clarify your objectives, with any new layout project, large or small, you have to face a particular limitation when you translate your ideas into actual scenic work. This is the limitation of space, both in width and length, that even the largest layout faces.

In real life we see distant hills miles away and know they are miles away. On a layout the distant hills may be less than 12 inches (30cm) away from our eyes, and furthermore their depth will be only the thickness of the card or paper backscene image. A real express train may be 12 coaches long. In OO gauge, 1:76 scale, a 12 coach train will be about 12ft (360cm) long and that is longer than quite a big layout of the sort that might fit into a spare room.

So when we come to build a layout of any size a degree of artful compromise is necessary to compensate for the space limitation without the compromises being too apparent. This is one reason why layouts based on actual locations are relatively few, and instead most modellers go for fictional or freelance settings, usually based on real companies and correct equipment but in settings that can be created - realistically of course - to occupy the available space. This is closely akin to what stage, film or TV designers have to do with scenery and settings, compressed to fit a stage, while looking totally convincing and realistic.

With model railways, this is why branch line, light railways, short line (USA), and equivalent settings in other countries are popular, for on these

Figure 2.1 On this very small 4ft 6in long layout a short halt with low platform served by a single unit diesel railcar was a necessary compromise to enable a passenger service to fit into such a small space. The shelter, lamp, and bicycle are from the Skaledale range.

Figure 2.2 Very effective scenic work in a small space by Julian Andrews on his Weston, Clevedon and Portishead Light Railway layout.

types of line, trains can be short, loco- motives small, and stations and rail facilities much reduced in size. There are a few visual tricks that help as well. One is what is called 'selective compression' of large buildings, keep- ing their appearance and purpose, but reducing the dimensions a little, like reducing a long warehouse by two or three bays, making lineside buildings 'tall but small', again with reduced length, using low relief, and reducing platform lengths. Station platforms, in fact, are one of the problems with compromise - a platform made to scale length will be too long for all but the largest layouts. But a branch line station platform three coaches long, around 3ft in OO gauge is a lot more practical. A good visual trick with short platforms to make them look longer is to keep them on the low side. In the old days platforms used to be lower anyway, and coaches often had a second footboard to allow for this. If you have ground level platforms, common on branches in Europe and America, you have a bonus, because the visual problem of a longish plat- form on a limited length layout is overcome. A few branch lines in Britain, notably on the GWR and GER, had small stations or halts with ground level platforms which is why the GWR

Figure 2.3 A selection of important tools for kit building, detailing and conversion work

diesel railcar has built in steps below the doors and the GWR autocoach has steps that can be lowered by the guard. All the stations on the LNWR (later LMS) Dyserth branch had ground level platforms too, and there were yet other examples.

Another visual trick when develop- ing the scenics on the layout is the 'vision blocker'. This is any object such as a building, clump of trees, rocky outcrop, a parked heavy lorry, cutting, etc, placed on the viewing side of the layout so that passing trains go momentarily out of view, either wholly or in part, and this has the effect of making the train's passage seem longer than it really is. All these limitations

need to be borne in mind when you start scenic work.

Tools and materials

If you are into the model railway hobby already you'll probably have a set of all the necessary tools needed for model and baseboard building. But for scenic work in particular it is handy to have a good pair of tweez- ers, modelling knives, steel rule, ruler and/or tape measure, small drill and/or Archimedes drill and spare drills. For smoothing or shaping plaster, etc, an old kitchen knife, plastic coffee stirrers, and wooden coffee stirrers are useful. Some art shops sell variously shaped tools for working with modelling clay, and old dental tools of various sorts can sometimes be found on sale, ideal for working on plaster finishing and shaping, though if all else fails an old kitchen knife and a few wooden coffee stirrers usually suffice, at least on small layouts.

You will also need a pot of white PVA glue and a tube or two of 'universal' glue, and polystyrene glue (or liquid cement) if you are using plastic kit parts.

In terms of materials you will find it useful to have plenty of balsa wood for everything from platform building to structure supports, barrow crossings over the track, or even for scratch-building small sheds, etc. Balsa wood is sold in larger model shops in 3ft (90cm) long 'planks' of various widths and thicknesses, and in 'economy' packs of assorted sheets and strips at a modest price. You'll also find balsa wood strip and hardwood strip very useful. Old egg boxes and cardboard from cereal packets, plus thick rigid card of almost any size is worth collecting for land-scape building - keep it all in a large marked cardboard box.

Next comes a selection of paints. For painting 'sky' effect on backscenes, and coating styrene hills as undercoat, ordinary emulsion paint is suggested. Get some light or 'sky blue' and white

for the sky and 'coffee' or other 'earth' shades for the ground. The small quite inexpensive emulsion sampler pots sold in hardware stores are recommended for this.

For scenic painting, acrylic paints are suggested, in particular earth brown, white, grey, light and dark greens, and black. Some large bushy art brushes are useful (14 or 12) for scenic painting and smaller (8,6, and 4) for weathering and other work.

Scenic materials

In recent years the availability of very high grade good quality scenic finish-ing materials has greatly increased.

Figure 2.4 Acrylic paints from three widely available ranges: Humbrol, Tamiya and Inscribe

Most model shops have a good selec-tion and many firms have big ranges. Quite a lot of 'water effects' kits are produced, and recent developments include miniature flowers of various sorts, garden vegetables, grass clumps, water weeds and much more, allowing

Figure 2.5 On this Hornby demonstration layout built by Nevile Read all the scenic material used is from the Skale Scenics range and shows its extent and realism.

Figure 2.6 The foreground trees here are made by adding foliage fibre to the tree armatures available in the Skale Scenics range. Trees behind are mostly from the 'Eco' range, including spruce. Canal bridge and boat are from the Skaledale range.

highly detailed work to be done. Trees abound, from generic low price items to highly detailed replicas of specific types in sizes to suit the most popular scales.

There are grass mats, too, of several types (of which more later) and even such items as 'grass' that can be sprayed from aerosol cans.

A few years ago lichen was used for scenic work, both for bushes and tree making. Rather good for its time, it is definitely replaced for realism by modern foliage material. There are some 'economy' items worth using, however. A very useful material is the green 'grass look' liner sold quite cheaply for lining hanging flower baskets. A sheet lasts for years and the material is ideal for shredding with the fingers and using as coarse grass, elephant grass, bushes, or even tree foliage. Some pet shops or departments sell plastic 'trees' for goldfish bowls and some of these can be used on layouts, at least in the background. Suitable garden twigs, or even dried out grape stalks can be used in conjunction with foliage material to make inexpensive trees to supplement more detailed ready-made ones.

Skale Scenics

In recent years Hornby have produced their own high quality scenic range with a huge selection to cover virtually every normal requirement. The entire range is extensive and is shown in the Hornby catalogue. There are ground cover materials in every possible shade of green, even taking seasons (eg, spring, autumn) into account in the variations. There are foliage fibre clusters, also in varied seasonal colours, which are ideal for undergrowth, weeds, creepers, young trees, and bushes. Long field grass, good for clusters or elephant grass, etc, is produced as is a huge selection of trees depicting actual species (such as sycamore, ash, etc), some tree kits, tree armatures (for 'home made' trees) and some 'eco' trees of both generic type and selected species (conifer, deciduous, walnut, etc).

Finally there is a series of 29 packs of gravel in every conceivable colour (including black, which could be used as coal or cinders) and three packs of rocks in different shades. References to Skale Scenics items appear in other chapters of the book, and they appear in many of the illustrations.

Spares box

In all previous books I've written I've made the suggestion that you should keep a spares box, collecting up all the left-overs from any kit-building or modelling you do. With most

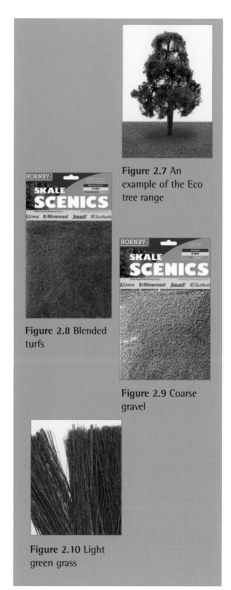

Figure 2.7 An example of the Eco tree range

Figure 2.8 Blended turfs

Figure 2.9 Coarse gravel

Figure 2.10 Light green grass

structure kits, for example, you might find odd doors, window frames, even printed signs or curtains that were not used. This sort of thing should be kept as they'll come in handy one day for another model. The same applies to tree kits, wall or fence kits, or whatever. As an example, spare wagon wheels may not look much use to you, but painted rust colour they can be added to the junk seen outside most workshops or on piles of scrap.

Even non-model items can be kept, such as tubing, old ball pen refills and much else. Veteran modeller John Flann has made many industrial buildings in his time, and all of them make creative use of oddments like nozzles of washing up liquid bottles as roof ventilators, old talcum powder containers as storage tanks, and much more in the same vein. At a lot of model shows, and in some model shops, there are often second-hand boxes with all sorts of oddments at low prices. Always check these out. You may find such items as street lamps, bits of wall or fencing, broken structure kits, bridge parts, barrows, figures, trees, and much else that may come in useful later.

For the same reason keep another box for any brick paper, embossed brick card, left-overs from card structure kits, miniature adverts and signs, plastic

Figure 2.11 Cheap plastic storage boxes are ideal for keeping spare parts, and the small drawers allow the parts to be separated into categories, such as doors, windows, wheels and so on.

card, good quality scrap card, and so on. You may want to divide these up into separate labelled boxes, and any unused bits can go back in the box. Any scenic backgrounds should also be kept in a box (or in a big folder) and any unused segments or any images useful for scenic work can be kept here too.

More storage

When it comes to scenic work you end up with quite a lot of storage requirements. Aside from keeping spare oddments, backscenes, and other items as noted above, it is a good idea to keep actual scenic material carefully stored as well. Most scatter materials - i.e. ground cover - foliage, and minerals such as coal, gravel, ballast, etc, come in bags or bubble packs. Once opened it is only too easy for the contents to spill out and be wasted or lost. My answer to this is to collect empty screw top bottles, such as 100g coffee containers, and jam jars with secure lids. Each pack is emptied into a jar, and a label is stuck on the lid giving the content name and make/reference number if particularly important. I keep these bottles in a shallow wooden box which can be carried to wherever layout work is being done. This sounds like a big task, but if you buy scenic material only as you need it, it can be a long term task as your selection of scenic materials builds up.

Trees and foliage in bubble packs or cartons are not so easily spilt, of course, and I usually keep them in their original packing. Where this is not practical I most often use freezer bags to hold them.

Jars or cylindrical crisp containers can also be used to hold balsa or hardwood strips and paint brushes or any other long items, an example being the girders, tubing, laddering and so forth in the Plastruct accessory range which you may use for detailing or converting. All these measures should ensure you have everything easy to store and readily to hand when needed.

Chapter Three

Keeping it simple

Keeping it simple

If you are a complete beginner to the model railway hobby, maybe starting with a new train set, or if you are encouraging a young enthusiast to make a start, some of the scenic modelling shown in this book may look too ambitious for you. It's true it helps to have modelling experience, but the best way to get that is to plunge in and have a go!

Unlike the trains and track, which are best not tampered with, you can always rework or replace scenery if you want a change. You may over time improve your modelling skills such that, say, you can now make better trees so you can change the original ones for new. Or you can add the telegraph poles you never put in place when the layout was built, and so on.

TrakMat

All the Hornby train sets come with a TrakMat (size 180cm x 120cm/6ft x 4ft) or a smaller MidiMat (size 160cm x 127xm/5ft 4in x 4ft 4in). The mats are fully coloured with ground effects and track bed in ballast finish. They give a very basic but imaginative scenic effect just as they come, and the track fits over the track bed, with the Hornby system of Hornby six further track packs allowing quite a big continuous circuit track layout to be developed. The mat is pinned or taped over a baseboard of the appropriate size.

Hornby make some neat accessory packs - station, engine shed, signal box, fencing, huts, signals, water crane, etc, in various combinations which fit

Figure 3.1 A layout built on a Hornby TrakMat with all accessory pack models in place and simple scenery (hills, trees, grass, etc, added).

in precise positions marked on the mat. You can add some trees and ground material later, and there is even room to fit some hills or rocky outcrops on the corners of the mat area, made exactly as shown in Chapter 9 of this book.

There is also a MidiMat provided with the 'Thomas and Friends' sets, with accessory packs (station, goods shed, tunnel, etc) to fit that. Some items, such as the yard crane, could also be used with other Hornby TrakMat layouts.

In short, if you want a scenically developed layout in the simplest way possible - or you are building a layout for a very young modeller – the TrakMat or MidiMat might be the way to go.

Light railway

The only real limitation with the TrakMat idea is that you are more or less committed to the track plan provided on the mat and supplied in the track packs.

If you want something simpler which gets closer to real scenic modelling, then a 'light railway' that uses the oval from almost any train set is worth making. In *The Hornby Book of Model Railways* I described the Westwood Light Railway, built on a 4ft x 3ft (120cm x 90cm) baseboard, for a keen young modeller. The building of this is shown and described in the previous book, but the track plan is repeated here with the scenic and structure features shown - all very simple - for anyone for whom this simple approach may be a new idea. One good thing about this sort of layout is that the track can be laid first with ballast effect on the bare baseboard, so that trains can be run immediately. This is important for a young modeller who does not want to wait for all the scenic work to be done before trains can be run. The scenic features and structures can then be added over whatever time scale suits you.

Also drawn here is the very similar Wright Lines plan, developed also from the idea of using train set track by the late Alan Wright over fifty years ago. As with the Westwood Light Railway, plenty of shunting can be done, as well as running trains around, and both layouts can be extended later on to another baseboard if desired. Scenic development on the actual Wright

Figure 3.2 Overhead view of the Hornby MidiMat with 'Thomas and Friends' accessory packs in place.

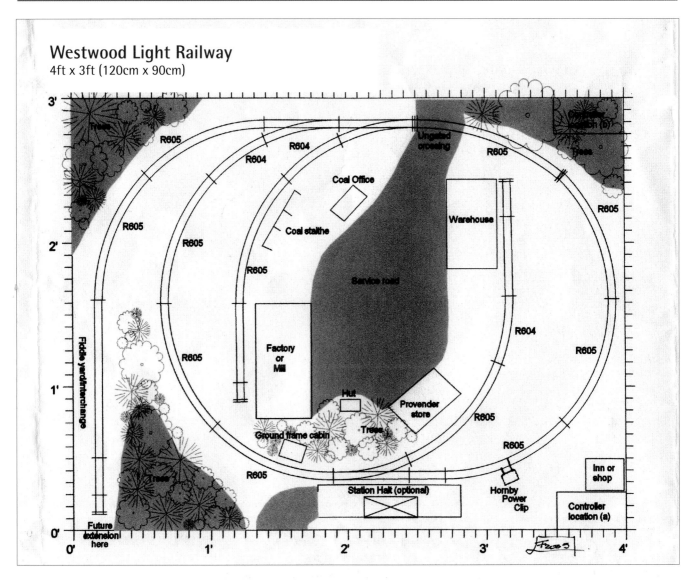

Westwood Light Railway
4ft x 3ft (120cm x 90cm)

Figure 3.3 The Westwood Light Railway track plan with Hornby track parts indicated and all scenics and structures marked.

The Wright lines track plan
4ft x 3ft (120cm x 90cm)

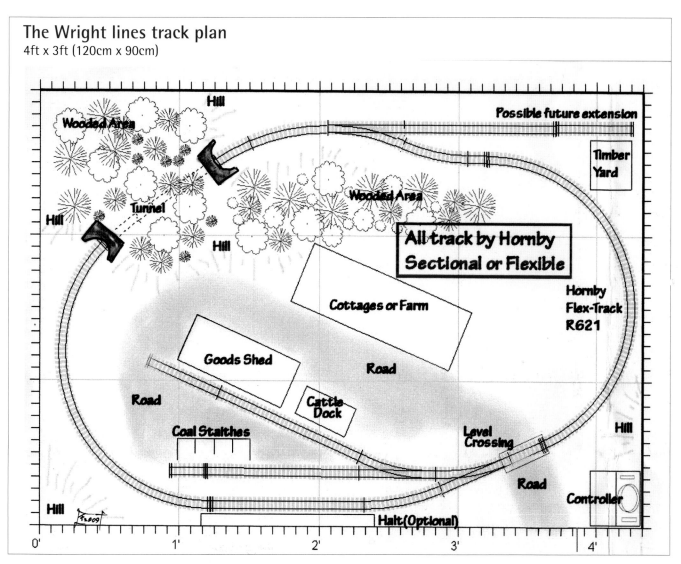

Figure 3.4 The Wright Lines track plan which operates in a similar way to the Westwood Light Railway. This plan shows it laid partly with flexible track (Hornby R621) but the actual layout can be altered slightly to fit variations in baseboard size. Scenic suggestions are marked.

Figure 3.5 Portable scenic items and light railway station on a bare baseboard showing how a simple 'junior' layout can get started. The coach is an old Hornby model no longer made.

Figure 3.6 Another set-up for a temporary beginner's layout, this time with portable hillside sections and Hornby International/Lima DB models.

Lines was more complex, including a tunnel and hill, but it could be done more simply at first until you gain more modelling experience. There are several possible variations on the actual form of the Wright Lines layout. It could be made up with a more regular oval shape than the version shown, and could be made to fit a slightly larger area if desired.

There are other very simple shelf type layouts possible which have been well covered in other books and model railway magazines - and some are shown in this book. From a youngster's point of view, however, they don't allow continuous running round the track, so for the easy approach to scenic work either for adult beginners or youngsters I commend the layout ideas suggested in this chapter.

Figure 3.7 Most modellers prefer spring or summer scenic settings, but autumnal settings are provided for. A few winter backscenes are available and a number of layouts have been built with winter settings. However, sprinkling loose imitation snow over the scenery is not advised - as it will spread everywhere - and any snow effect should be glued in place in the same way as grass scatter material.

Chapter Four

Backscenes

Scenic flats and backscenes for layouts

A successful model railway layout is in some respects similar to a stage or TV set. Within a small area the impression must be given of a real world, so that the viewer's interest is captured and the imagination fired.

Of course, a model railway layout is only as good as the sum of its whole, but a lot can be achieved simply by giving apparent depth to what are actually very limited dimensions. A shelf-type layout, for instance, may only be 15cm (6in) deep, but it is possible to make it look much deeper by providing a convincing backscene, as would be done on a stage or TV set.

Some of the simplest techniques require only the use of an ordinary paint set. The paints can be water colours, posters, oils, acrylics, or even household emulsions, though it is best not to mix the different types. **Figure 4.3** shows one of the simplest tricks of all suitable for an 'out in the country' setting on a narrow shelf layout. Assuming you attach a hardboard or plywood scenic backboard to the rear edge of the baseboard, then your first move is to paint the backboard as blue sky, using quite pale blue and white.

Figure 4.1 A Bilteezi printed background in use, on a hardboard backscene which has been painted with 'sky' effect. At left is part of a Bilteezi card cut-out factory used as a scenic flat glued to the backscene. At the lower edge some 'grass and weed' colour has been painted in. At bottom edge can be seen the holes drilled to allow the finished backscene to be attached to the back edge of the baseboard.

Figure 4.2 On this N scale layout a store shed cut from a model catalogue illustration has been glued over the printed Bilteezi back scene. The office building is from the Hornby Lyddle End range, and Skale Scenics vegetation is used in front of and at the edges of the printed backscene to give a good illusion of depth even though everything here except the office is flat on the backscene.

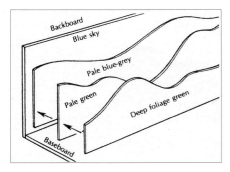

Figure 4.3 A backscene constructed from card layers as described below.

Paint it on horizontally, rather darker towards the top, with white paint streaked and run into it to lighten it towards the bottom. Variations could include a touch of grey if you want a winter sky, or a little pink, which, if not overdone, gives a warm hue to the sky.

When the backscene paint is dry, use old card (such as the inside faces of food cartons) or thick lining paper and cut three rows of undulating hills. You could, if desired, shape the highest of the three as mountains rather than hills. Paint the three different layers pale blue-grey, pale green, and deep foliage green, and glue them in layers to the backscene. This is the simplest way of making a backscene with apparent depth, particularly if you have only limited artistic ability. The use of layers is actually more effective,

also, than simply painting the hills in place on the backscene. If the base-board is wide enough, some modellers space the layers 2-3cm apart, a matter of choice.

As a digression, the importance should be emphasised of the variation in colour of the hills. Because of atmospheric conditions distant terrain looks 'bluer' and generally lighter than close terrain. This you can verify from observation. Hence when reproducing terrain on a backscene the hill colours are graded as outlined above to get a similar effect of distance.

It is possible to buy from model shops, pre-printed backscenes. In many cases they provide a complete artistically painted terrain. These are easy to use, but because they are readily available they become very well-known and familiar on all too many layouts. Hence a 'home-made' variation, unique to your layout, may have appeal to those who seek something more original.

There are many ways of using commercially available backscenes, however, to give something different from the material as presented. The backscenes themselves may be cut and re-arranged so that they no longer exactly resemble the original printed version as sold.

In Great Britain there are the Bilteezi and Peco ranges of scenic sheets which actually include a sky background (if you don't want to paint one yourself), and hill and terrain sections which may be cut and glued in layers to the sky background. In Europe the German company of MZZ offers a similar range, and another British producer is Townscene.

A further variation on this theme is to cut suitable parts from magazine, calendar, advert, or travel brochure illustrations for overlays in the same way. If you look around you will see many examples of illustrations in colour which may have a use in model railway scenic backgrounds. The main requirement is that the illustration should be matt. Glossy illustrations will reflect light and thus destroy any illusion of realism. It is possible to spray suitable, but glossy, illustrations with matt clear varnish if you are happy to spend money also on the aerosol of matt varnish. This will overcome the reflection problem but needs practice to do successfully.

Once the basic terrain is depicted on the backscene you can add all sorts of foreground features, also in the form of overlays. For example, trees can be painted separately or in groups on stiff paper, and cut and glued in

Figure 4.4 A very typical card cut-out of a warehouse from the German Sipp/Auhagen range, easy to fold and glue but still needing bracing before adding it to a backscene.

Figure 4.6 Illustrations from suitable model boxes or model building catalogues can be cut out for scenic use. Typical is the Hornby Skaledale Water Works building from the model carton (at top). Below it is a backscene made up of a printed Peco sheet with three structure cut-outs overlaid in the foreground. In the centre is a Skaledale gas works building. When on the layout, Skale Scenics hedging and undergrowth will be added at the bottom, concealing the lettering that remains from the model box.

Figure 4.5 Some printed cut-outs can be used to make a complete backscene. These Bilteezi 'occupied' arches, two sheets, were used to form a neat background to a small goods yard 'inner city' layout. Note that the doors have been opened up on the left-hand arch and the area inside is painted black to form a 'void'.

Figure 4.7 A typical building flat from the German firm of MZZ, depicting old city centre structures. At top are optional trams and a kiosk which can be cut out and glued on the front as overlays.

Figure 4.8 Even trees can be purchased as printed strips for overlaying on other backscenes. These evergreen trees are from the Horizon range (made in Canada), and simply peel off the backing for application as desired. They are self-adhesive. Also in the range are deciduous trees, mountain ranges, and other useful scenic features.

place. **Figure 4.10** shows the simple outline and method of painting them. However, you can, again, cut suitably sized trees from colour illustrations and pre-printed backscenes, or even from model catalogue illustrations, and glue them in place. Painted trees are also available to add to backscenes. Structure illustrations can be similarly cut out and glued individually to a flat backscene.

Structures as part of a backscene are almost always very effective. Several firms, including Street Level Models (UK) and Walthers (USA) produce realistic printed OO/HO size buildings as scenic flats, and examples are shown here. Sometimes it is possible to combine a low relief structure with a scenic flat so that they all appear to be part of the same building. For example, a covered loading bay is fully modelled over the railway track, while the rest of the factory is depicted solely by a flat cut-out stuck on the backscene. Many of the card cut-out buildings available, such as those made by Bilteezi, Metcalfe, Superquick, Sipp (Germany) or Alphagrafix, can be adapted additionally as scenic flats merely by cutting out individual front or back walls and gluing them to the backscene. These adapted flats lack perspective, of course, but as they are

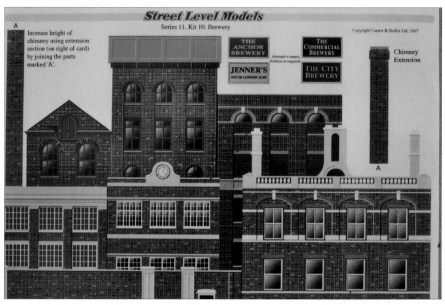

Figure 4.9 Many colour illustrations can be cut out or adapted, to be used as overlays or within backscene montages. Here are three examples (from top to bottom) a birthday card, a travel advert, and an old calendar page.

Figure 4.11 A leading producer of good scenic flats in Britain is Street Level Models, and this is one of their biggest productions, a complete brewery. Note that a separate tall chimney is provided and four different name boards. The entire structure must be cut out from the printed sheet and glued to the backscene.

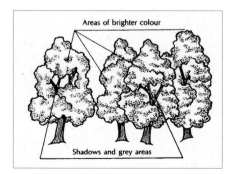

Fig 4.10 A guide for printing trees on a backscene

full scale for your model they are best used to depict immediate background structures alongside the railway. Parts of plastic kits can be used in a similar way. Another technique is the use of a specially taken colour photograph. This is quite feasible if you own an old SLR camera, or a good digital camera. Find a small building you want on the layout, photograph it front on in good cloudy bright or light sunlight weather, and ensure there are no vehicles or people in the way. You may need to get a print to the size you need from a conventional negative, and for an average building an ordinary enprint gives more or less the correct scale for N and a 30% enlarged print matches HO. These are the ordinary options offered by the photo processor.

With a digital image you have many more options, such as enlarging to any size or even using Photoshop techniques to add more doors or windows

Figure 4.12 With a digital camera you can produce scenic backgrounds based on actual locations. Veteran modeller Jack Chipperfield photographed this picturesque Scottish fishing village of Pennar in very fine weather and has printed it out in two sizes here, one scaled for N gauge and the larger one scaled for OO gauge.

Fig 4.14 One of a good number of flat cut-out buildings from the American firm of Walthers, scaled for HO, and called Instant Buildings by them. On this sheet are an old iron foundry and an American-style coal merchant.

Figure 4.13 The MZZ range is unusual in including winter versions of many of its backscene sheets, such as this city street. The snow and ice on the buildings is printed on very realistically, but the lamp and snow-covered street are added by the modeller here.

Figure 4.15 'Western USA' style scenic flats from the Walthers Instant Buildings range, as cut out and ready for use.

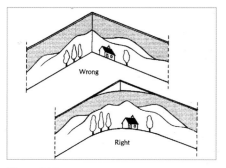

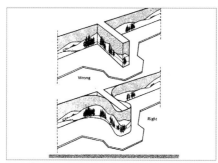

Figure 4.16

Figure 4.17

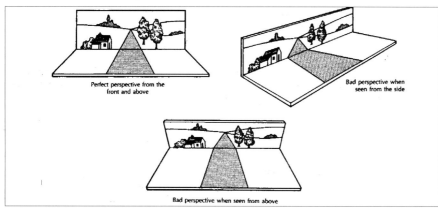

Figure 4.18

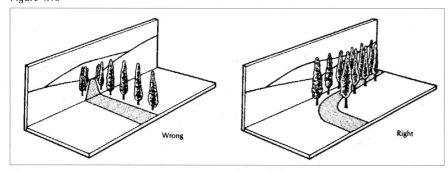

Figure 4.19

Figure 4.20

or even an extra storey, depending on the software you have available.

Points to remember

There are several 'tricks of the trade' that help to make any sort of back-scene or scenic flat arrangement more effective. **Figure 4.16** shows the best treatment at corners - curve the back-scene around it. If for any reason you can't, use a clump of trees in the corner to disguise the right angle. A varia-tion on the problem is shown at **Figure 4.17**. Again plenty of model trees in front of the backscene at that point, with higher ones in the actual corners, would be an alternative treatment.

Importantly, when gluing scenic flats and backscenes to the backboard it is essential to make sure that there are no air bubbles trapped underneath which cause unrealistic bulges later. Use an art roller, an old rolling pin, or a jam jar to ensure the backscene is very securely and evenly glued.

As noted earlier, with scenic back-grounds we are creating an illusion of distance - or, at least, attempting to do so. In this connection there are often minor problems to overcome. One of the most common is perspective. This is not much of a problem if the backscene shows only countryside or a town, but when you come to depicting a road disappearing into the distance you may encounter the visual problems shown in **Figure 4.18**. In theory a road in the foreground should merge smoothly into the road continued on the background, but in practice it is difficult to maintain this illusion, however much you try. A better answer to the problem is shown in **Figures 4.19/20**. Instead of trying to depict the road on the background, curve it round in front of the backscene and 'lose' it among the trees.

Whenever scenic flats, either depicting structures or distant hills, are to be glued into place check the cut edges. Very often they show white and it will spoil the illusion if the white edges are visible. Use a suitably coloured fibre-tip pen to colour the cut edge to closely match the printed colour before the scenic flat is glued down.

Making the transition between backscene and modelled foreground so that it looks plausible is also important. A wall, fence, hedge, or bushes along the base of the backscene is a common ploy, visible in some of the illustrations here. If the ground is higher between the backscene and the track bed, a low embankment might be used along the gap. Choose the transition to suit the setting. Low relief buildings might also be used, as described in Chapter 11.

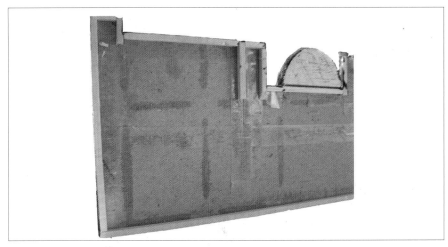

Figure 4.21 The back of the scenic flat buildings shown in Figure 4.15 showing that they are glued to thick card, then braced with wood strip to ensure that they stay perfectly flat and do not warp any time in the future. This is an important safeguard for all card structures.

Figure 4.22 An example of the type of backscene available as printed sheets.

Digital solutions

Modern developments have in recent years added new possibilities to the creation of effective and realistic backscenes. As noted above you can photograph any attractive building with a digital camera and print it out to size, possibly also altering details with Photoshop techniques. The only obvious need is to photograph at ground level and straight on so that you do not end up with a different perspective from the rest of the backscene.

However, with a digital camera you can do more than that if you can get a good eye-level panoramic shot of a large area suited to your backscene requirements. A simple example shown in **Figure 4.12** is the Scottish fishing village Pennan which modeller Jack Chipperfield photographed in perfect weather, then printed it out to OO scale size, but did a smaller version, too, for N scale. The finished prints - on matt paper - can then be cut to depth and glued to a backscene board just as for the more conventional printed backscenes sold by model shops. There is even more potential here if you are adept at computer techniques. As an example, professional modeller Brian Taylor has a large scale layout called Pelporro, and the backscene here is

Figure 4.23 Making a basic backscene. A strip of hardboard or thin MDF of the desired depth is first painted 'sky' colour down to baseboard level, using suitable shades of light blue and white emulsion paint for choice. The printed background design of your choice is carefully cut out and glued to the board using white PVA glue uniformly applied, taking care that it is straight - a pencil line at baseboard level helps you line it up. Then use an art roller to roll it perfectly flat, eliminating any air bubbles under the sheet. A round bottle or other round object, like a rolling pin, could be used if you do not have an art roller. Some backscenes include the sky, but an option is to cut away the printed sky and paint the sky on the backboard as has been done here.

made from a photograph of the picturesque fishing village of Polperro in Cornwall. But to suit the length of the backscene Brian duplicated one or two of the buildings and moved some rooftops, and so on. A similar technique was used by Andrew Knights for his German HO layout set in a fictional - but plausibly modelled - suburb of Cologne. He took several pictures across the rooftops (from his hotel window) of the city centre and joined

them digitally to give a convincing view of the distant city behind the suburban station and apartment blocks modelled on the layout. Again some of the roof tops were craftily duplicated to fill out the required length of the backscene. These techniques are increasingly popular with a lot of layout builders today.

Moving on from this you can also access websites around the world that provide images of buildings of all kinds, from skyscrapers to freight depots, that

Figure 4.24 The small Contor Yard layout, 4ft long in HO/OO, built by the author, is only 8 inches wide and has most of of its buildings as scenic flats on the background. The factory on the left is cut from a kit catalogue. The warehouse on the right is from a Townscene printed background, and the goods yard wall is from Skaledale retaining walls glued direct to the background board. The GWR 'Terrier' and wagons are by Hornby, as is the old Scammell dust cart in the foreground.

can be downloaded and printed out to the required scale, either to be cut out and glued in place like the pre-printed scenic flats, or else combined with other downloaded images to make up scenic lengths, such as an industrial area or a background village. Scenic King and Railroad Graphics (USA) and Modellgrafik (Germany) are among a good many organisations providing this service.

Finally there are other firms producing CD (or DVD)-ROMs which you can purchase and, again, access and download images to your required scale which can be printed out for backscene use. All subject areas are covered. For example Busch (Germany) have a 'Harbour' DVD which gives ships, dock-side cranes, container cranes, all types of ship, warehouses, and more which you can mix and match for a harbour layout.

Chapter Five

Hills, contours and terrain

On a very small narrow shelf layout, you may be able to depict most of the landscape on the backscene with just a little scenic work needed, in the form of vegetation (bushes, trees, undergrowth, etc) or rough ground on the baseboard itself adjacent to the tracks.

But on a layout of any size, in particular with good width, you'll need to model a much fuller version of the terrain in the form of actual hills, embankments, cuttings, and so on. There are several ways of doing this, largely using readily available scrap material, so the cost for the basic terrain building can be very low. On most layouts the hills or land at the side of the track has to be modelled.

The conventional way

In what may be called the 'conventional' method, a basic ground shape is formed to give the required contours, and this is completed by covering it with a plaster type surface that can then be given the final scenic finish to replicate the natural ground cover, growth, and vegetation – see **Figure 5.1**.

To provide vertical support, usually from the baseboard edge, a vertical board, which can be from plywood or hardboard, is cut to the desired contour shape and affixed to the

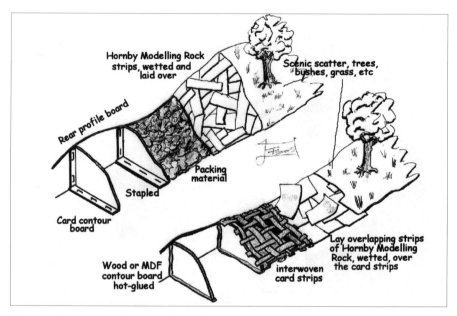

Figure 5.1 Alternative methods of making built-up landscapes using either packing material such as old newspaper (top) or interwoven card strips (bottom) to support the ground surfacing.

baseboard edge. Some modellers use very thick rigid cardboard for this job, the sort found in most sturdy shipping cartons. Assuming the track is already laid, mark the edge where the terrain is to come. You can use more thick card to make contoured supports, and then pack the inside with screwed up newspaper or broken bits of styrene foam packing. Broken up egg box pieces can also be used. Over this you need to put strips of card to support the surface material.

Essentially all you do is cut a lot of strips 12-25mm wide from old breakfast cereal boxes and make a criss-cross pattern to what ever gentle contours you need. These are glued, pinned, or stapled into place. Over the criss-cross you lay strips of scrim, a material used in dress-making that you can usually buy at clothes or tailoring shops. You can do all this yourself, but some firms make it even easier by producing packs of pre-cut strips and scrim for instant use. Over the scrim you simply paint (with an old paint brush) a layer of modelling plaster, and only a thin

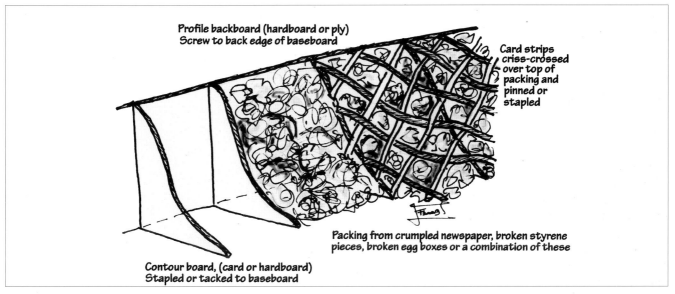

Profile backboard (hardboard or ply)
Screw to back edge of baseboard

Card strips
criss-crossed
over top of
packing and
pinned or
stapled

Packing from crumpled newspaper, broken styrene
pieces, broken egg boxes or a combination of these

Contour board, (card or hardboard)
Stapled or tacked to baseboard

Figure 5.2 A closer view of the basic method of building large lengths of lanscape area. This is for hillls seen from only one side. but for hills 'in the round' the work must be duplicated each side of the profile board.

application is needed. It all dries as a light hollow shell. Add some brown or black powder paint to the modelling plaster when you mix it to 'kill' the whiteness of the plaster so that later chips or cracks won't show up stark white. Once the plaster is dry, paint it ground or grass colour, ready for scenic finishing later. The term 'modelling plaster' here covers several materials. A number of model firms sell modelling compound in packs to be mixed for use. Some include 'rock' colouring material. Some modellers use what

is often called 'patching plaster' sold under various trade names such as Polyfilla and available in DIY shops.

Alternative surfaces

Though the scrim method is well-proven, there are alternatives which you might find easier. An old established method of covering the contours is to use old newspapers cut into small squares or rectangles, held over the criss-cross supports and secured by painting them in place with water paste liberally applied. Apply patches

until the whole surface is covered with paper, if necessary with more than one layer. Leave it to dry out and you should have a fairly rigid surface.

The second method is to use thick good quality kitchen roll paper (the cheapest discount price type is too thin), instead of newspaper and use this a sheet at a time, brushing over each sheet with quite a thin mix of modelling plaster. Again more than one layer of paper is usually required, and it must be left to dry out before proceeding with scenic work.

Figure 5.3 Modelling Rock (R8070) is a quick and easy way to form landscape contours. It is a plaster-impregnated fabric which is wetted first. When dry it can be painted in scenic colours and textured with scatter material in the usual way.

Figure 5.4 Modelling Rock (R8070) is very versatile. Here it is being used make the rough ground behind the small station shown in Figure 2.1, applied to the baseboard surface.

A third alternative is my favourite and, though slightly more expensive ,it is quick, much less messy, and sets superbly with a good surface texture. This is essentially bandage type material (very like scrim) impregnated with dry plaster. Several companies in the scenic business produce this under such names as ModRoc or Landform. Hornby produce a very good version under the name Modelling Rock (R8070).

As soon as you dip a piece of this material in a bowl of water, the plaster is dissolved and you can simply stretch the section over the criss-cross supports and leave it to set hard. Then take another section and repeat until the whole area is covered and you have the finished hill. If necessary use more than one layer. Leave it all overnight to set hard and you can then paint and glue on the surface vegetation detail as required.

The R8070 Modelling Rock is actually very versatile indeed. You can use it instead of mixing plaster for almost any sort of basic ground covering. I have used it to make low hillocks or shallow cuttings by using scrap balsa wood or bits of styrene packing glued in position on the baseboard and then covering it with a Modelling Rock section, moulding in the desired shape with my fingers as the plaster dries. I've even used this material to depict rough flat waste land, as you might find in the corners of a goods yard. The sheet of Modelling Rock is simply wetted and pressed down on the baseboard, being shaped in ruts and ridges, etc, with the fingers as the plaster dries. Given all these ways of utilising this type of plaster impregnated bandage, the extra cost is well justified.

If none of the work involved in

making up contoured terrain in the way described appeals to you, it is worth mentioning that the German scenic firm of Noch makes a system called Terra-Form, consisting of varied lengths of strong thin wood strips which can be plugged together with plastic clips to form the framework for any desired shape and contours of the terrain. Scrim, plaster bandage or other surfacing can be applied over this in the ways described above. While quick and easy to do, it is quite expensive compared with all other methods described here.

Using expanded polystyrene

If you have only a small layout much of the raised or rough ground area around the track itself can be depicted simply and easily. The ground areas concerned are the low banks you might find even alongside level track, or infilling around sidings and level crossings. On a HO/OO layout much of this may be no higher than 15mm and covers only small areas alongside the tracks. It is hardly worth mixing messy plaster to do this, and a better alternative is to use styrene foam pieces.

Styrene foam comes as packing material very frequently these days - even Hornby models come in styrene foam 'trays'. You don't need to break

Figure 5.5 On some shelf type layouts, pieces of expanded polystyrene may be all you need for depicting low hills or banks alongside the track. These are shaped and glued in place. White PVA glue is being painted on here for a grass matt to be added over the polystyrene shape.

these up, and should not, for they hold the models safely. But a great deal of styrene foam can be found elsewhere as packing for all sorts of items, and most of it is thrown away. There are also ceiling tiles and other decorative pieces in this material and it is safe to say that everyone can find some scrap styrene somewhere. This material can be cut easily with a craft knife or even an old serrated steak knife. Pieces can be cut to shape, trimmed and 'sloped' as necessary to give a natural effect, then pinned or glued to the baseboard in the desired positions. After this the

styrene is painted in 'earth' or 'grass' colour with acrylics or other water-based paints, and when the paint is dry you simply sprinkle on scatter material over a coating of glue in the usual manner.

Styrene foam has the advantage of being very light, easy to work, and easy to glue. There are some key rules, however: (1) Always spread newspaper on the table top or on the floor while cutting and shaping is done to catch any small grains of styrene. A major problem is that when cut some small pieces crumble away and if they are

Figure 5.6 Layers of expanded polystyrene pinned and glued together to make a low hill on the Westwood Light Railway layout. Note that the upper layers are shaped to form the desired contours.

Figure 5.7 Pieces of wet Hornby Modelling rock being used to make the surface covering on the polystyrene hill shown in the previous picture.

not caught (wrap up the paper and throw it away when work is finished) the tiny granules will carry all over the house and cause unpopular cleaning problems. (2) Only use white PVA glue (or pins, or pins and glue) to secure the styrene pieces in place. Any other glues will dissolve the styrene. (3) For the same reason only use water-based paints for colouring. Oil-based paint may dissolve the styrene. (4) Always ensure all the exposed surface of the styrene is thoroughly painted. This 'seals' the styrene and stops any future crumbling.

On a very small narrow shelf-type layout where space for scenic effects is, in any case, limited, you may be able to do all the terrain work with styrene foam.

More uses of expanded polystyrene

Expanded polystyrene is a potential fire risk, but when coated with modelling plaster or thick emulsion paint this risk is greatly reduced, and the surface finish then matches terrain modelling in the conventional style already described.

Slicing polystyrene makes a mess of granules, however, so cover the floor and table with old newspaper to collect the debris as noted above.

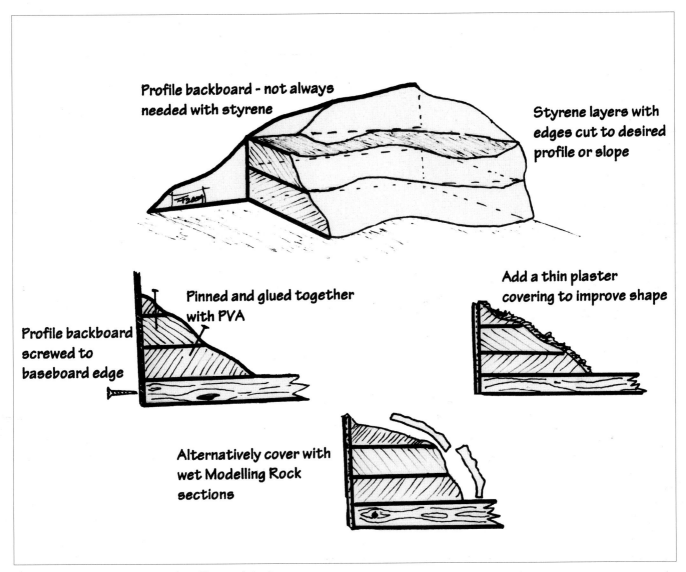

Profile backboard - not always needed with styrene

Styrene layers with edges cut to desired profile or slope

Profile backboard screwed to baseboard edge

Pinned and glued together with PVA

Add a thin plaster covering to improve shape

Alternatively cover with wet Modelling Rock sections

Figure 5.8 Scenic landscape construction with expanded polystyrene.

The principle is easy enough. Just build it up in layers to give a contour effect as shown in the diagrams. Pins, nails, or glue secure the layers. When the glue is set, simply cover with patching plaster or modelling compound as shown here. Modelling Rock strips are even more effective for this.

Note that large blocks of polystyrene may be cut complete to form cuttings, etc. This latter technique can be very effective and quick, as shown here. Long strips of styrene used to pack such items as TV sets or washing machines are particularly useful, and they can often be found discarded in skips. You can tailor the shape to suit the site by judicious carving and slicing. Segments as long as 3ft (90cm) can be carved and shaped, and obviously more sections can be butted to the first if you need a longer stretch of terrain.

Once carved to the desired shape, coat the entire segment all over with matt brown or earth coloured emulsion paint. To save money, buy the small sample pots of emulsion sold in hardware stores rather than a large can. The choice of colour is not too critical, but earth colour is useful because if any scenic dressing falls off later on the earth colour will show through rather than the white of the styrene

Figure 5.9 Though scenic coverings are dealt with in the next section, this shows that a styrene terrain section can be at least partly worked on with scenic material before it is put in place on the layout. Here a start is made on sprinkling the grass scatter material into a coating of glue over the earth coloured styrene.

foam surface. The emulsion coat also stops any of the styrene edges crumbling away and reduces the risk of melting in the unlikely chance of a fire or unexpected heating. Vertical or near vertical areas where grass would not grow and rock may be exposed can be painted 'rock' colour.

Once the paint is dry the unit can be positioned on the layout and glued or pinned to the baseboard. You can then get on with the scenic covering, dealt with in the next section, but it is equally possible - and actually easier - to do the main scenic covering on the segment before you put it in place on the layout. Note that using large

styrene segments like this eliminates the need to put a contour backboard along the baseboard edge, unless you want to take a 'belt and braces' approach which might be useful, for example, if the layout is often moved about as might be the case if it is taken to model railway exhibitions. The backboard in this case will save the styrene block from accidental damage.

Figure 5.11 The completed section of hillside is now being coated with earth coloured matt emulsion paint, well worked in to any crevices. The vertical area where a bare rock face will be seen has already been painted grey. Rest of the area will be covered with grass and vegetation.

Figure 5.10 Making a complete cutting section from a single block of expanded polystyrene salvaged from packing material. Note the old kitchen knife used for shaping the block and use of old newspaper to collect the trimmed pieces. Broken off pieces of styrene are being glued and pinned on top of the main strip and cutting and shaping is proceeding along the length of the strip.

Figure 5.12 Styrene pieces, cut to shape, glued in place as 'infills' between points and backscene in a goods yard and being painted to depict a low rock cutting.

Chapter Six

Texturing, vegetation and trees

Figure 6.1 On this Hornby demonstration layout by Nevile Read, all the material used for the attractive setting comes from the Skale Scenics and Skaledale ranges.

Once the backscenes are set up and the hills and landscape are in place, we come to the need to depict the details of the terrain being modelled. This amounts to adding the grass, bushes, trees, undergrowth, and other features, which might include flowers, vegetables in gardens and allotments, crops in fields, and waterways of all kinds (dealt with separately in the next chapter). Man-made features such as tunnels and bridges are included in the landscape building, but roads, paved areas, hedges, fences, gates, stiles and similar small details might best be included at this stage.

Scenic material for all this is widely available from a number of makers, and every model shop has a selection. Hornby have the Skale Scenics range which alone will suit the needs of most modellers, though there are some items not included in the range at the time of writing that are in other makers' ranges.

Track ballasting and weathering

The track, and the track bed, is part of the scenery on a model railway layout, even if you don't often think of it as such. If you had shiny track straight out of the box pinned down to the bare baseboard, then built fully scenic

Figure 6.2 The track was weathered with dark earth paint before laying. With the track and foam ballast in place, a dirty black/brown wash of acrylic paint is applied over the ballast strip to remove its 'new' look.

landscape all round it, the end result would look peculiar to say the least.

So the first consideration is to weather the track - that is make it look like real track soon after it is laid, which is usually a dullish brown, sometimes black-brown, with only the top shiny where passing wheels keep it clean. You can usually weather sectional track before it is pinned down which is generally a quicker job. Whether you do this or choose to lay the track first, use a matt dark earth, preferably acrylic, to paint the sides of the rails,

then also paint over the sleepers so they also look dirty and no longer like shiny black plastic. On points, avoid painting any of the contact strips or the inner faces of the moving parts. Paint acts as an insulator if it gets on electrical contacts and it can also cause the moving parts to 'stick' if too much paint is put on the sleepers below the moving rails. Also take care when painting round the rail connectors, ensuring no paint gets inside. When the paint has dried use a track rubber to clean the top surface of the

rail back to its shiny appearance.

Some common methods of ballasting are summarised here.

■ Foam ballast This is sold in the Hornby range, and others, and has moulded recesses for the sleepers and is in earth colour. It is easy enough to use, though care is needed when pinning down the track through the ballast not to pin the track too deep into the ballast. The idea should be to let the track 'float' in the ballast, keeping all level with the depth of the strip itself. To ensure the sleepers don't 'lift' out of the foam, however, it is a good idea to put a small amount of white PVA glue under the sleeper strip before fitting the track to the ballast.

To take away the 'new' look of the foam, paint it over with a black-brown acrylic wash. A problem with foam ballast is that it can crumble and decay with time. However, this seems to happen mostly if the layout is exposed to daylight for much of the time. I have a layout over twenty years old with foam ballast that is still perfect, but it is a portable layout which, when not in use, is kept in a tall dark cupboard. If you don't have this facility the only answer would be to lift the track

Figure 6.3 'Brush-it-On' ballast after application. An old dental tool is being used here while the ballast is still wet to remove pieces that would jam up check rails and the moving parts of points.

Figure 6.4 'Brush-it-On' ballast used with fine scale Code 83 HO track on the author's German St Kathrein layout, showing the realistic effect possible.

and lay it again with new foam ballast strip.

■ Brush-it-On ballast This is a ready-prepared ballast which comes in a bag with an adhesive which is activated when water is added. The track is positioned, pinned down, and weathered. The wetted ballast is then literally spread over and around the track bed and left to dry. Ballast graded for N, OO/HO, and O is available in several colours. The process sounds simple, and it is. But there is quite a lot of work to do afterwards because it is necessary to remove any ballast left on top of the sleepers, ballast stuck in check rails, and any ballast threatening to gum up the points, and it must be done with care. It can also be quite a messy process until you get used to it.

■ Bonded ballast This is the most usual way of ballasting. Dry ballast is brushed and shaped around the track and sleepers, then a 'wetting agent' - water with a drop of washing up liquid in it - is dropped over the ballast, followed by a drizzle of very much thinned down - to watery consistency - white PVA glue. This dries transparent and holds all the ballast in place. Again care is needed not to leave ballast in check rails, on sleeper tops, or gumming up the working parts and contact areas of points.

■ Bogus ballast   Also described in the previous book, this uses one of the Hornby scenic sheets R8066 or R8067 cut into strips of ballast width and placed under the track when it is pinned down. There is no actual ballast used, but the optical effect is good, particularly if a few weeds are glued in and around. As it happens there have been quite a few examples spotted (in USA, Canada, Germany, and even on some British light railways) where the track really is laid on a thin ballast base and the ballast is not carried deeper to bed in the sleepers.

■ Gummed ballast   This is a variation, slightly more complicated, of the bogus ballast idea. Here you need ordinary parcel tape wide enough to match the trackbed. The parcel tape is stuck under the sleepers, gummed side up so the sleepers stick to it. Pin down the track or points a few sections at a time. When a suitable length is laid, use fine grade granulated cork ballast and spread it over

Figure 6.5 Conventional bonded ballast is seen on this small goods yard layout which also has unmetalled roadway between the sidings.

Figure 6.6 Bogus ballast used on an American layout with Hornby track and Hornby R8067 fine granite sheet. Note weathered track, weeds in siding, a log 'bumper', and embossed card paving on left.

the track bed. The cork ballast will stick to the gummed parcel tape and give a very good appearance. Shake off any loose granules on to an old newspaper and return these to your ballast pot. The visual effect is good, and it seems to last well. I have a layout built in 1985 where the ballast looks as good as ever, though again the layout is stored out of direct light which may help.

Ground covering

From the ballasted track bed we can now move on to the surrounding terrain. Remember, however, that an area of several feet or metres is left clear alongside the outer edges of the ballasted track bed, usually in the form of a cinder or earth path so that track workers can walk the route clear of the track and passing trains. Hence any terrain with grass or foliage should start reasonably clear of the track. Years ago enthusiasts used to make their own 'grass' scatter material by dyeing sawdust, or dyeing surgical lint grass green. Today, with an abundance of well textured and nicely coloured ground cover scatter material available you hardly need consider the old methods. In the Skale Scenics range alone there are 15 shades of green plus 8

Figure 6.7 Gummed ballast, using parcel tape as the basis, and here used with fine scale track on an EM layout.

blended shades, four of them autumnal. Most are spring or summer shades.

The most usual method of grassing an area is to paint the prepared landscape surface grass green, then when it is dry, paint a section with either a diluted PVA white glue (mix it with a little water), or ordinary office type water gum, which is my preference. Then simply shake the ground cover evenly over the gummed area, ensure there are no gaps, and leave it to set. If anything err on the generous side.

A few points to make here. First, as noted earlier, I put scatter material into labelled jars, as they are easier to handle than in packets. Second, I use

small plastic spoons of the sort given in ice cream tubs as a way of shaking the ground cover over the glue. But others use old pepper pots filled with scatter, and also old kitchen sieves. But the Skale Scenics range includes a low price shaker (R8906) which I have started using as well as the plastic spoons. It works well.

If you want only a thin grassy surface, as on scrubland for example, paint the ground surface earth colour instead of grass green and scatter the ground cover thinly so that the 'earth' shows through. An option throughout is to use two or more shades of grass scatter to give good visual variation.

Figure 6.8 Laying hedging (R8044). It is glued in place using with PVA glue.

Figure 6.9 Scatter material is most easily applied to large areas with an old tea strainer.

Figure 6.10 Applying ground scatter the conventional way

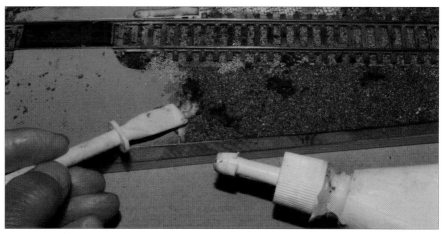

Figure 6.11 Ground covering in process. White PVA glue is being spread in places where specific grass effect is needed.

Figure 6.12 Using the 'bonded' method of scenic scatter application, the material is dropped into place loose and dry.

Figure 6.13 Skale Scenics shaker suitable for simple and effective dispensing of ground cover turfs and gravel.

Figure 6.14 Painting an embankment and trackside area with earth and grass colour prior to adding the ground cover. Note weathered track, bogus ballast, and backscene in place. For this low embankment, shaped expanded styrene packing material is used.

Figure 6.15 Using tweezers to add weeds and long grass round a buffer stop base. Note also the low hedge in the background, also made from teased out foliage material.

Bushes and undergrowth

It is customary to leave ground cover overnight to dry, but in practice I find it practical to glue foliage, such as bushes or undergrowth, in place over the grassed areas while they are still drying and, of course, this speeds up the work. Invaluable for this are Skale Scenics foliage clusters, done in 15 shades, 6 of them autumnal. R8839 dark green medium is good for ivy type growth, but shades go down to light green, and a selection is useful to have.

Other makes of similar material give varied textures and shades, and I also use green basket liner, intended for domestic use, but good for undergrowth and long grass, etc, being simply torn, shredded and broken up in the fingers.

Figure 6.16 An ice cream spoon is being used here to put the ground cover in place over the glue. Note at right a paved area depicted by embossed cobble sheet.

Exactly the same goes for green pot scourer pads, treated the same way.

For areas of weeds or clover clumps, etc, Skale Scenics ground cover tufts or similar coarse ground cover from other ranges can be used.

As with all model work you can't beat observation of the real thing to get the idea of how undergrowth can grow and spread and how trees develop. Take the chance to look at embankments and retaining walls to see how grass, bushes, and undergrowth look on your next train journey!

Grass mats

Grass mats are very useful and these days are realistically textured and also done in seasonal or other variations such as autumn grass, summer grass, rough moorland, and others. For lawns, grass verges, parkland, or even smooth downland hillsides they can be cut and glued in place. Only lawns or tennis courts would be entirely flat. For other locations, such as trackside, bits of thick cork or balsa can be glued to the baseboard surface first so that the grass mat, when glued down undulates a little. Hornby produce mats in light green (R8064), dark green (R8065), and meadow green (R8068) all in slightly different shades. These are very smooth mats and good for depicting any mown

Figure 6.17 Undergrowth can conceal unwanted features. This board-mounted point motor is being disguised as bramble bushes with foliage clumps, but ensure no glue or foliage obstructs moving parts.

Figure 6.18 The kit used to make St Kathrein station on the author's German HO layout had a cracked and chipped end wall. The damage was disguised with foliage fibre arranged like ivy climbing up the wall. Note brickwork and platform paving with coursing picked out, curtains added in windows, and station master using the platform telephone (F), an added detail.

well-kept grass areas such as lawns, tennis courts, bowling greens and such like.

Whatever ground covering you use, ensure that all structures are 'bedded in' to the ground, most easily done with grass or weeds around the bottom of buildings or buffer stops, etc. A gap around structures can ruin realism.

Trees

Today trees are easy if you have no great modelling skill or the time to make your own. All makers of scenic accessories and many kit makers, too, offer high class trees of every possible species and size to suit all the most popular model scales. Some are at premium price, of course, but the answer here is to use these in the foreground or in prominent positions, with background trees from the lower priced sets, or your own home made trees. Even palm trees are available in some ranges, ideal if you are modelling a layout set in southern France or California among other locations.

Using Skale Scenics foliage fibre clusters (or similar) it is possible to make your own trees, with suitably shaped and textured twigs from park or garden, or using dried grape stalks. Skale Scenics also offer tree armatures to allow you to do the same thing with foliage of your choice. Twigs can also be used for fallen trees, often seen in woodlands, and don't forget that undergrowth tends to spring up around these trunks, and grass and weeds grow around the base of tree trunks, which means you need to do this as well when you drill out locating holes in which to 'plant' your miniature trees.

The generic cheaper trees, 'Eco' trees in the Skale Scenics range, can be used

Figure 6.19 Excellent use of grass mat sections for verges round an office block. Note also embossed sett sheets used for the roadway around the building. Foliage fibre is used to depict ivy climbing the wall

Figure 6.20 A large open area, in this case a station yard, being represented by a scenic mat, the grey tarmac mat (R8066) in this case, secured with white PVA glue.

Figure 6.21 Extensive use of grass mat to depict lower mountain slopes on a German HO layout. The support for it here is the Terra-Form framing from the Noch range. Note access here (at back of layout) to the tunnel interior.

Figure 6.22 An example of professional trees, Oak from the Skale Scenics range.

Figure 6.23 An example of professional trees, Scots Pines from the Skale Scenics range.

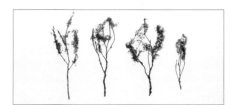

Figure 6.24 Wire foliage branches from the Skale Scenics range.

Figure 6.25 A deciduous starter tree kit. Tree kits include a coated armature which can be bent and formed to the desired shape together with three shades of foliage for maximum effect.

Figure 6.26 Use of economy trees, partly as a 'vision blocker' but mainly to disguise the join between two baseboard sections. This is on a SR layout by Stuart Robinson. The train is just visible through the trees. The join is just apparent in the backscene boards at the top of the picture

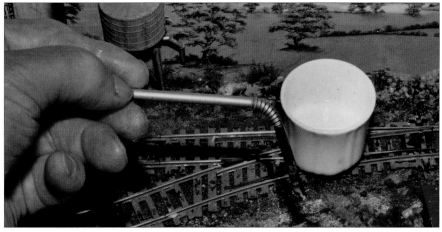

Figure 6.27 Using a drinking straw as a pipette to run diluted PVA glue over an area finished with loose gravel and undergrowth. When dry, everything here is fixed in place. Bonded ballast is glued in place the same way.

in the background mostly or in woodland clumps. There are apple trees (R551) and shade trees (R553) long in the Hornby range, and cheap fir trees by several other makers. Some cheap trees don't really have a textured leaf effect, but this can be added by brushing the 'leaf' area with white PVA glue and rolling the tree in green scatter material in a foil tray or jar, giving a good visual improvement when dry. I have found that with all the cheaper trees, including the Hornby 'Eco' type, it is possible to convert them to low relief merely by cutting off all the foliage one side of the trunk, using sharp scissors. This leaves you, in effect, with half a tree which can be glued to the backscene, or even alongside a low relief structure. It is worth pointing out, too, that bushes, undergrowth, and trees can cover problem areas, such as defects in structures, and joins in baseboard sections in particular. Trees can also be used to help conceal hidden sidings or the point at which the track runs into the hidden sidings, effectively behind a screen of trees.

Other details

In Britain all railways have to be fenced off. The exception applied to certain light railways and some tracks in public roads. In most other countries fenc-

Figure 6.28 The Eco tree range is ideal for those who have a need for a large quantity of realistic trees at an economical price.

Figure 6.29 The cheapest type of model fir tree can be improved by painting it with white PVA glue and dipping it into scatter material.

ing is not needed unless, for example, a farmer fences off a nearby railway to stop cattle wandering on to the track.

Fencing, if needed, is best done while the grass and undergrowth is added. Quite a few varieties of fence are available, mostly in plastic of the post-and-bar type, and needing to be glued into holes drilled in the ground surface. You may need to cut it and adjust to follow contours. It looks good to make the odd break in the bars or give it a 'tumble down' look in places. And remember grass or weeds sometimes grow higher up the post and creepers can grow along the bars. Farms adjacent to the railway will also need fenced and gated

fields, and both farms and roads may need hedges, strips of which are available in some scenic ranges.

Weeds, gravel, rough stone surfaces, scree, and so on can be found all over the place. Weeds and growth in rail sidings are a nice scenic feature. I find this is best done the way we do bonded ballast. First place all the coarse weed (or gravel, or scree, etc) in or around the track, and between the sleepers in the case of track, then use a pipette to drop 'wetting' agent (water with a drop of washing up liquid added) into the weeds or scree, etc. Follow this at once with diluted PVA glue (a lot of water, little glue) and leave it to set overnight.

Figure 6.30 Bedding in a structure. White PVA glue is put around the base of this American HO water tower, with teased out foliage (in the mince pie tray) being positioned with tweezers.

Figure 6.31 The same scene completed with all foliage in place and also between the tracks.

You could use a real pipette, but you can equally well use a drinking straw used like a pipette. Lastly, when you have finished a scenic session there will actually be some loose unglued scatter material on the layout, maybe ballast or gravel too. With a small portable layout you can spread a newspaper on the floor, then stand the layout on its end so any loose material falls on to the newspaper. A larger layout is best built in sections so that each module can be worked on separately, with loose material gathered in the same way. You can ditch the loose material that drops on to the newspaper if you wish, but I gather even this up and return it to a jar for future use.

Roads and paved areas

Most layouts have goods yards with paved areas in them, and roads may lead to your station, alongside the track, or over the hills. In most cases the whole yard area is on the level with, possibly, a retaining wall or rising ground out at yard limits. There is usually a flat pathway or roadway between the sidings so that staff, mobile cranes, road vehicles, etc, can get among the rolling stock.

This 'flat' nature makes the scenic work quite quick and easy in miniature. The yard area roadways and surface level in general is usually level with the top of the ballast so that road trucks can back up to wagons or vans for direct loading/unloading. In some bigger yards, notably in city or town areas, some of the sidings may have

Figure 6.32 Using modelling plaster, with added grey paint, to depict rough unmetalled roadways in a goods yard (with some low bank from broken cork sheet being covered in the foreground).

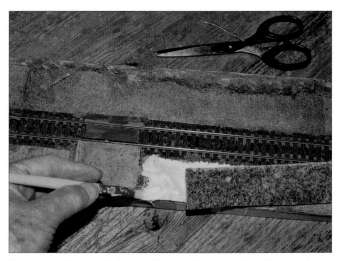

Figure 6.34 Grass mat being used for a trackside area alongside a road crossing, with white PVA glue used to fix it down.

Figure 6.33 Using paper templates to work out accurate shapes for roadway sheet (by Merkur) being used for a road and level crossing.

Figure 6.35 Shredded basket liner used for rough long grass along the bottom and top of this low relief cutting. The moulded cutting sheet was first painted with 'rock' colour.

proper tarmac roadways built up to rail top level and paved over between the rails, as in a level crossing, so that road vehicles can cross between sidings, as can fork lift trucks used for handling the wagon or van cargoes.

In essence, therefore, in modelling terms you need to bring up the roadway level to ballast height (or rail top height if a paved-in effect is needed) and there are several ways you can do this depending on the depth of ballast base you need to match. Some German firms (including Merkur) actually make sheets of moulded styrene roadway with various paving stone or sett patterns incorporated. It is possible, however, to use balsa sheet or thick card to bring the ground level to the desired height and use embossed or printed card cobble, sett, or paving sheets glued on top after cutting to shape. To make sure the area alongside or between the tracks is accurately cut - avoiding mistakes in cutting the card to correct shape - it is a good idea to make a paper template of the area trimmed as needed to fit, then trace the outline on the printed card to get a perfect fit of the area.

The same technique is used to make a level crossing over the track with the approach roads at track level. If you use magnetic couplers it is a common

Figure 6.36 Roadway made from card textured with grey paint and a little plaster or model compound powder. Balsa strip is used for the middle of the road crossing. Note warning signs for ungated crossing.

Figure 6.37 Grass mat strips are here being cut and used for verges along the roadside and tracks of the layout shown in Figure 7.33.

trick to place an uncoupling magnet as the centre part of the level crossing paving between the rails. If you don't do this, use the card paving instead or a suitable strip of balsa sheet.

While the above suggestion assumes you are using cobbles, setts, or paving as the yard or road paving, modern yards and roads are usually finished with plain asphalt surfaces. For this you can use ordinary matt surface card such as the inside faces of cereal boxes.. You can also use this to surface balsa wood platforms if you like. Again the card is cut to the desired shape and once in place it can be painted. I normally use a medium grey shade of acrylic paint, and while it is still wet brush in the odd stroke of dark earth or even black on goods yard surfaces or busy roads. An option which gives an even better texture is to sprinkle and mix some plaster powder into the paint (which is decanted into a foil mince tart holder), and this gives quite a realistic finish, notably on areas near the front of the layout. It is not worth doing on distant roads.

It is worth mentioning, too, that some German companies, including Noch and Busch, produce roads in rolls, complete with road markings, and mostly self-adhesive and curvable. Several types are available, all

Figure 6.38 Painting over a balsa sheet platform with grey paint with added plaster powder (in spoon) to give an asphalt texture.

Figure 6.39 Flexible roadway material in various styles for HO and N from the German Noch company.

pre-coloured, and sized to scale for HO (also suits OO), TT, N, and Z.

Lastly, some yards or roads are unmetalled with just a rough earth or stony surface, sometimes rutted as well. This is best depicted with modelling plaster, or patching plaster such as Polyfilla (or similar) mixed in a bowl with grey or brown paint added (to kill the whiteness). Then it is just 'painted' over the area to be treated and 'textured' with wheel marks or shallow ruts as it dries out. For uneven surfaces glue bits of card, cork sheet, or balsa sheet to the surface before painting on the plaster mix.

Figure 6.40 Using Skaledale retaining walls to depict walls round a small inner city goods yard layout, and about to be glued to the backscene.

Figure 6.41 Foliage fibre clusters have been used as creepers to hide the join in the retaining wall sections. The roadway is of painted card with gravel being used to hide a join in the card.

Chapter Seven

Modelling water

Depicting convincing water effects in miniature can be done in various ways, some simple and some more complex. If you are not confident about making water areas, you can easily avoid settings where water is featured. However, water can be a very attractive component of the scene, and where a harbour or canal lock or basin is modelled it can add to the operating potential of your layout, with quayside spurs and sidings plus cranes and warehouses, to add a lot of extra interest and an excuse for busy shunting as cargo is transferred to or from ship or boat.

Commercial aids

Several firms in the scenic business offer quite extensive ranges of water effect kits, some for still water and some for rough water such as rapids or waterfalls. Most have a clear acrylic base (which may also need to be mixed with hardener) and some come in granular form which has to be dissolved first. Appropriate colours (blue, green, brown, etc) are generally provided. With these water effect kits you normally have to model a river bed or pond bed first, or the rocks around a waterfall or rapids. Then you pour the mixture in place and leave it to set hard. As it sets you can usually work

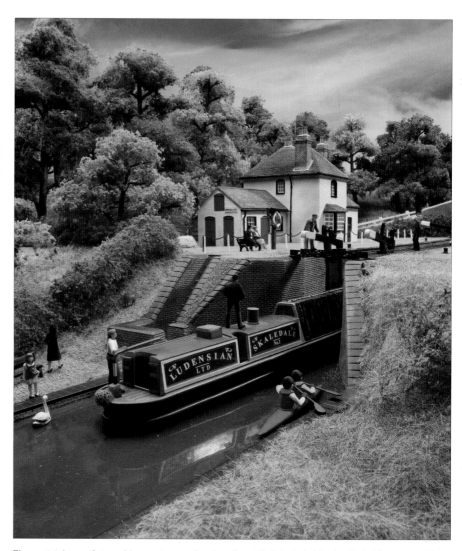

Figure 7.1 A complete and impressive canal series of models is included in the Skaledale range, with canal boats, lock, bridge, lock-keepers cottage, store, and upper and lower ends of the lock, all shown here, with SkaleScenics trees beyond.

Figure 7.2 Rough running water from Noch Water Gel being shaped around the river bank with a stiff paintbrush, as the Gel sets.

Figure 7.3 Water Gel by Noch allowed to set smooth with water lilies and bulrushes, etc, added.

in ripples, waves, or foam effects with an old brush or spatula. These kits are easy to use, though some are quite expensive. Examples of what can be done are shown.

One or two firms also offer 'lake film' which is intended for large open areas such as a lake, pond, or harbour basin. The Noch version has transparent blue film with wave or ripple effect moulded in 41cm x 26cm or 75cm x 50cm sizes. These sheets are simply cut to the desired shape or size and pinned or glued in place. A version from Kibri has a sheet of blue-green thin plastic with a clear rippled sheet that is glued over it once the desired shape is cut.

Obviously with all water effects you have to do related scenic work, such as a sandy beach, rocky shore, lake or river bank and so forth, even driftwood floating on the surface, to develop the realism. Some scenic accessory makers in recent times have also produced (for HO/OO) aquatic plants like bulrushes, reeds, water lilies, etc, to add to the realistic effect, while you may want to add fishermen, swimmers, paddlers, boats, or picnickers, etc, to the scene.

'Do it yourself' methods

If you have only got space on a small layout for minimal water effects like streams, small ponds, puddles, a small

Figure 7.4 Noch Wildbach (brook) water used to model a fast-running river.

ponds, is to model the actual pond bed, complete with rocks, waterweed, etc, then use a sheet of stiff clear plastic or acetate glued on top to represent the water surface. The edge of the sheet is concealed with grass, reeds, etc.

For puddles I have used either gloss clear varnish or clear 'universal' glue blobbed into puddle-size recesses and left to set. Add a second layer (or more) to make the puddle deeper. I have represented small roadside streams or springs tumbling down a hillside by carving out the channel first and dribbling clear glue down it, leaving it to dry. Again, repeat the process a few times until the depth or width of the stream is to your liking.

Quite often seen in real life are pipes, conduits, or culverts where water is channelled into a stream or gully. You can use a piece of plastic piping (such as a piece cut from an old ball-pen barrel) for the pipe. For the running water pouring out, find a clear plastic sprue - the frame that holds the glazing parts in a plastic building kit - and hold this at each end (very carefully) just above a candle flame until it softens and can be bent. Cut out a segment each side of the bend, glue one end in the pipe, and you get the effect of water pouring out. This is shown in **Figure 7.11**. The same technique (with

boat landing area, or a jetty, there are easy ways to depict water. One of the oldest ideas, dating back over 70 years, for depicting rippled or slow- moving water is to model the area - pond or river - in plain smooth card or plastic card, paint it gloss blue/green or brownish depending on setting, then glue crumpled cellophane over it with small dabs of clear paste or white PVA glue on the river surface to hold the cellophane in place - the glue dries clear. Small waterfalls can also be depicted by cellophane stretched over a card base, with gloss white paint streaked down it and dabs of white paint to give a foam effect.

Another method, best for small

Figure 7.5 A canal lock and narrow boat always attract attention on a layout. Roy Hickman models the scene perfectly, with fine trees and vegetation. Hornby produces a canal bridge in the Skaledale range.

Figure 7.6 The view upstream. Hornby have made canal scenes like this in 00 scale much easier by introducing a lock, canal sections, canal basins, a butty boat, canal keeper's cottage, and accessories.

Figure 7.7 Making a small water inlet at the edge of a small layout. The 40 thou plastic card sheet is glued in place.

Figure 7.8 The jetty sides, in this case timber, are added, the water area is painted and varnished, and the boat is in place. Mooring ropes, bollards, and rubbing strakes are yet to be added.

Figure 7.9 River modelled from an acrylic water set by Andrew Knights. Note nicely detailed river bank with fenced off railway line and good use of figures.

Figure 7.10 Quayside scene on a German N gauge layouts, with train, jetty, road vehicles and boat. The railways models are from the Arnold range.

varied diameters of clear sprue) can be used to show water pouring from a tap, hydrant, village pump, or drainpipe, and it can even be added to a ship in a harbour setting to depict cooling water pouring out into the harbour.

Quickest and easiest

Despite all the ways of representing water described above, most modellers, myself included, use the 'paint and clear varnish' method. Small layouts don't usually have much room for a large area of water, but some sort of harbour inlet, ferry boat landing, canal basin, river section, pond, or stream can often be included. The water area in each case is modelled with a smooth, flat surface. Plastic card 40 thou thick is ideal. Thick smooth artboard or foamcore is also suitable but it is essential that it is well braced with a support underneath so that the surface stays perfectly flat. If it warps or twists the illusion of a water surface will certainly be lost!

With the water surface in place, it is then painted the desired watery colour in *gloss* model paints. This may be dark blue mixed with green, a lighter blue, brown mixed with black even, depending on where the water is supposed to be. If you don't think the first effort looks right, try again varying the mix. For canal basins or ponds, etc, I find dark blue with a little green works well. For sea inlets a lighter blue looks good, but this is a personal view, for the individual modeller.

Figure 7.11 Modelling a water culvert. The water pouring from the pipe is from clear plastic sprue, and touches of white paint depict the 'bubbles' on the water surface. The water is depicted by the 'paint and varnish' method. Note the 'muddier' colour nearer the banks.

Figure 7.12 Canal basin modelled on the author's German HO St Katherein layout, with water by the 'paint and varnish' method. Embossed stone card is used for the jetty side, with vertical baulks.

Figure 7.13 A canal basin on a seaport layout built by the author, with two Hornby Skaledale canal boats alongside the jetty. Note details on the jetty, low relief warehouse and the Peco harbour backscene.

Figure 7.14 A nicely done beach with water from an acrylic water kit. Note how the colour is made lighter as it gets shallower.

With the paint fully dry on the 'water' area, now give it a coat of gloss clear varnish and leave that to dry. When this is dry repeat the process at least four times but better still 6-9 times. Leave each coat to dry out before applying the next. Illustrations here show examples of this work done on several small layouts.

As modelled the feature usually depicts a canal, river, or even small harbour basin or landing. As you are only modelling part of it, the rest of the water area does not really matter as it is left to the imagination like all the 'rest of the world' not on the baseboard.

There is much variation possible in size, the example shown in **Figures 7.6** and **7.8** is only 45mm wide and 180mm long on a HO/OO layout, yet it is still big enough to look busy and it will hold a cabin cruiser, sailboat, or small fishing boat easily without looking too small. Other pictures show larger basins on larger layouts; in fact dimension it to suit your own requirements.

If your water area is supposed to be a pond or river, you then need to model the adjacent banks in the usual way. If your water area depicts some sort of harbour or canal basin, then you need

to model the jetty or quay sides, using wood, embossed brick or stone card, or plastic brick or stone, as desired. The illustrations show typical jetty or quay-side construction.

If you want to model rough water, such as on the seashore or in an exposed harbour, one way to do it yourself is to use a plaster mix (either patching plaster or modelling compound), spread a thin layer over the water area, and then work in wave shapes as the mixture dries and stiffens. It can then be painted blue-green with gloss paint, adding white tips to the wave edges. Then apply several coats of gloss clear varnish as before.

With any of these methods of depicting water, any other details such as drift wood, water weed, figures, etc, can be added last of all.

Chapter Eight

Rocky surfaces

Rocks and mountains are popular on model layouts. They are spectacular scenic features, and they give an excuse for the steep gradients and cramped situations prevalent on many small layouts. Obviously they also provide an excuse for the tunnels or deep gorges giving access to hidden sidings and fiddle yards.

There is quite a wide interpretation of what constitutes a rocky terrain. It doesn't necessarily mean high mountains. There are plenty of lowland areas where there are rocky outcrops. More commonly, however, a mountainous area is modelled. To give an illusion of depth a scenic background depicting mountains can be used on a shelf layout, with only the foreground actually modelled in relief. Firms such as Peco (UK), Faller (Germany), Walthers (USA) and others all produce mountain backscenes depicting terrain from their respective countries.

If you build an actual rock face, however, it is best to go for height and bulk to make it believable. A small mound, however rugged, will not be so convincing as a craggy cliff-like depiction of part of a mountain.

The rock often appears only as outcrops from a grassed surface. In its simplest form the rocky outcrops can be modelled from broken pieces of

Figure 8.1 Good and bad examples of rocky terrain construction. On the right is a plausible version with rocky outcrops visible. On the left is a less plausible example with less believable erosion depicted and the rocky outcrops randomly placed.

Figure 8.2 A rock cutting made from a moulded plastic rock sheet, in this case glued to a hardboard backing. It also conceals an exit line to a fiddle yard behind the cutting. Note judicious painting to give a rock effect, and the added vegetation along the top and at the bottom.

Figure 8.3 Cork bark is here being used to depict a rocky outcrop. It is also used in a near vertical position to depict rocky cliff faces.

Figure 8.4 Small hills and banks can be shaped from polystyrene block without any plaster covering. The light green here is 'undercoat', to be painted and textured later.

Figure 8.5 Making a rock face above a tunnel mouth, using modelling plaster that has been pre-coloured with grey acrylic or powder paint.

expanded polystyrene stuck into a wet plaster surface prepared as in Chapter 6, or the rocky surface can be worked into the plaster covering as it dries. A stiff paint brush and a scriber of some sort can be used to give the rocky cliff surface as the plaster dries, cutting ledges and strata layers by horizontal working with the scriber.

Moulded rock sheeting is available and would be suitable for small surfaces, particularly of the vertical type. Cliff faces or cuttings, however, are very easily depicted by cutting and/or layering polystyrene blocks and giving a coating of modelling compound as required.

A favourite method, much used for rocky faces, is cork bark, sold in some model shops and also by florists. Cork

bark is also included in the Hornby range in small (R8046) and large (R8047) packs. Most of this bark has a realistic striated surface that looks remarkably like a rocky texture. Obviously this is easy to use, and is often big enough to be free-standing if a gorge or cliff face is to be depicted.

It is possible to mould your own realistic rock face. One way to do it is to use crumpled kitchen foil and press it on to the modelling compound while it is drying. Removing it in good time before the plaster sets will give a good 'rock face' texture caused by the creases in the foil. Some modellers have used casting resin to make cliff and rock sections, with pieces of coal or real rock used to make a master surface in the rubber mould. This gives an excellent

and realistic effect if you can master the technique.

I have also used the versatile Hornby Modelling Rock (R8070) to depict rock faces. The name suggests it is ideal for modelling rock faces, even though it can be used for any sort of ground covering - hillsides, rough land, etc - as described in Chapter 6. The rocky cliff faces I made were simply done by draping lengths of wetted Modelling Rock over very roughly shaped styrene blocks. These were contoured along the top edge and cut to a steeply sloped side. The Modelling Rock placed along the steep sides was shaped and moulded with the fingers as it dried out to suggest the layers of strata and a few ledges. Then it can be painted 'granite' or 'chalk' colour as desired.

Figure 8.6 Making a small section rocky cutting outcrop using 1cm deep styrene sheet in this case. The layers have been glued and pinned together and painted with thick emulsion.

Figure 8.7 First task is to paint in greyish shading to depict the bare rock faces.

Figure 8.8 Scenic work on the first section as completed, with grass on the ledges, and grass and rough undergrowth on the top, all added in the usual way.

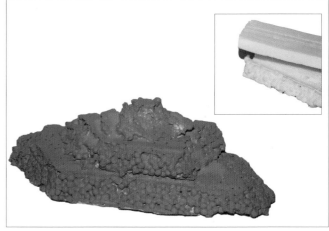

Figure 8.9 The second separate unit made up and coated with emulsion. Bits of the original styrene sheet can be seen in the inset box.

Small sections

There is another way of making rock effects that is pleasingly simple and particularly good for small layouts, even for temporary table top set-ups. For this we still use expanded polystyrene as before, but the rocky sections are made in small units separately rather than be built into the main scenery. Some examples are shown here, both of them using styrene sheet 1cm thick in the first example and 1.5cm thick in the second example, though the thickness is not too critical if it suits the effect you are aiming for. The width of the segments is not critical, either, and they can be made to suit a specific site. The first example shown is a typical stratified rock face, made in this case from four layers, with the bottom one sliced to cant upwards, with the next three layers glued and pinned above it. The second example is just a rocky outcrop made from three layers of 1.5cm thick sheet, each layer carved to a slope and glued and pinned. Both the examples are about 4½ ins long (14cm), but they can be any reasonable length, even twice as long if desired.

When the basic assembly is completed it is given a generous thick coating, overall, of 'earth' colour emulsion paint (actually called 'Coffee' on

Figure 8.10 Only a single piece of expanded polystyrene block was used to make this rocky outcrop on a very small 3ft (90cm) long N gauge layout made by the author. The block was simply carved to shape, painted with emulsion, pinned and glued in place on a lakeside edge on the layout, then given scenic treatment. All the scenic material used was from the Skale Scenics range, including the tree foliage, though the tree trunks were made from old grape stalks. Figures here are by Preiser and the boat is adapted from a model ship kit lifeboat.

Figure 8.11 A top view of the previous scene shows how the rocky outcrop was arranged to conceal the track as it runs off into a fiddle yard. Skale Scenics rocks are used to depict harbour wall protection.

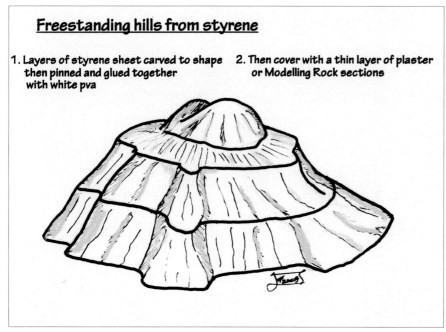

Freestanding hills from styrene

1. Layers of styrene sheet carved to shape then pinned and glued together with white pva

2. Then cover with a thin layer of plaster or Modelling Rock sections

Figure 8.12 This drawing shows the basic way of making up simple free-standing outcrops as shown in Figures 8.6 through to 8.11.

my pot but any shade roughly earth coloured will do). After painting the 'rocky' edges with greys, browns, etc, to depict granite or sandstone or chalk, the only remaining task is to add the vegetation, which includes grass and undergrowth on the ledges and flat areas, with a few small bushes, etc, as desired. This added vegetation will cover up any ugly joins in the styrene layers.

Note that these units are built on your work top away from the layout itself. This makes it much easier and less messy to work on them. On a small shelf type narrow layout they might suffice if simply placed in front of a hilly or mountain backscene, but on a larger layout they can be built in to the scenery at any appropriate point and, of course, you can make the unit to the size you need for your particular layout. Now apart from this, the small sections are free-standing and very

light. This being the case they can also be used on temporary layouts, or on junior layouts, such as those using the TrackMat in Hornby train sets. Even a temporary test track set up on a short plank of wood starts to look more realistic if you stand two or three of these portable sections behind the track.

Real rocks

Also worth considering is the use of real pieces of rock in scenic work. However, by this I do not mean large chunks as you might use on a garden rockery. I mean very small pieces of suitable size which can be built into the scenery. I have done this quite often, usually with very small pieces. Just keep an eye on gardens, parks, and even beaches where tiny pieces of suitable shape and fine texture may be recovered and incorporated into your setting. For example, I have added small pebble-size pieces along the foot of rocky hillsides, suggesting they are rocks that have fallen down from above. Even smaller grit-sized pieces can depict scree from minor landslides down a mountain. I have also seen some nice layouts in Welsh settings that have made great use of slivers of slate to give a very realistic slate quarry. The Skales Scenics range actually includes packs of small rocks (pebble size) (R8829-31) in off-white, brown, and dark brown colours. One use I made of these is shown in **Figure 8.11**, depicting rocks dumped along a sea wall or dam wall as part of the erosion protection. These, and sharper small pieces of stone, could also be used as rocks along the waterline or below cliffs in coastal settings.

Figure 8.13 A tunnel through rocky mountain terrain on a German HO layout. In this case the rocky surfaces have been done by skilled work with modelling plaster over a basic ground shape.

Figure 8.14 All the scenic arts are shown in this German HO layout view with a well modelled rock cliff behind a country lane and houses.

Chapter Nine

Tunnels and bridges

Though tunnels, bridges, and other engineering structures in general are covered separately here, the requirements need to be considered before you start scenic work and even at the planning stage for the layout itself. For that is when you get your first ideas for the sort of landscape you want to model, and any lakes or rivers to be crossed by the railway, roads to be bridged, and so on. And obviously the tunnels, bridges, viaducts, or whatever else you plan, have to be built in as the scenic work proceeds.

In this connection it is worth pointing out that it is not necessarily essential to have a tunnel on a layout, for the real railway engineers have always avoided the expense and extra work involved in tunnel building wherever they could. On lightly used cross-country and branch lines, and light railways, they often diverted the route to follow the lowest contours specifically to avoid having to tunnel through hills. If you give your layout a 'low lying' scenic treatment, you can forget about the problem just like real railway engineers.

However, tunnels are great features on any layout, and they not only add drama but can have operational value as well. For example if you have a layout with storage tracks or a fiddle

Figure 9.1 Superb tunnel building on a German layout, using a moulded tunnel mouth and wing walls. Note that the inside walls of the tunnel, where visible near the tunnel mouth, have also been modelled. The mountain terrain and vegetation is also expertly modelled

yard behind the scenery, the models can exit and enter the scenic area of the layout through tunnels in a very realistic way. If your layout has rocky or rugged terrain, tunnels can be used to good effect to take the track through spurs or outcrops, just as on real railways where there is often no

alternative in mountainous areas.

There is only one snag in describing tunnel building and that is the huge variety of possible tunnels. Almost every layout will have its own requirements depending on the size of the layout and the type of scenery you build. If you want to play safe, a very

Figure 9.2 Retaining walls alongside the track are often needed in mountain areas, as nicely modelled here on the same German HO layout featured in the previous photograph.

Figure 9.3 Typical British tunnel on the OO gauge Melbury GWR branch line layout of John Flann. Note the smoke staining above the tunnel mouth. In this case the tunnel is a dummy in that trains run through the tunnel mouth to or from the hidden fiddle yard the other side of the backscene, which is a common way of hiding the fiddle yard or storage tracks on many layouts.

short tunnel through a rocky outcrop is a pleasing feature, not least because you can usually get your hand into a short tunnel to recover a derailed train, and to clean the track from time to time. This is actually an important consideration, and if you build a long tunnel you need to make allowance for access to the interior, either by making a section of the hill above the tunnel removable, or having an open slot on the non-viewing side. This enables you to get at any train that derails or stalls inside the tunnel, and also to clean the track as previously noted.

At this point it is worth mentioning the traditional 'toy train' free-standing tunnel still made by a few firms, including Hornby who have such a tunnel (R9224) in the 'Thomas and Friends' range. These are short tunnels with a scenic top finish that can just be placed over the track as a temporary structure and can also be used with the Hornby TrakMat. It is ideal for youngsters or temporary table top layouts. But you can also use this type of short tunnel on a permanent scenic layout, too, by fixing it in place and then building plaster scenery as required over the top of it. The value of these short tunnels is that they break up your line of sight of the train, and any 'vision blocker' that does this

Figure 9.4 Use of the Skaledale tunnel mouths are shown here on a large layout, with both a single line and double track tunnel mouth in use and retaining walls along the hillside cutting.

Figure 9.5 A road bridge built from a kit of parts on one of the layouts built by the late Dave Howell. This is also used to conceal the entrance to the fiddle yard which is on the far side of the bridge. There is a high degree of detail, including nicely done banking, an advertising hoarding, iron railings, a gas lamp, and a bus crossing the bridge.

Figure 9.6 Railway Bridge R8570

Figure 9.7 Girder Bridge R657

Figure 9.8 Brick Bridge R189

Figure 9.9 Viaduct R180

Figure 9.10 River Bridge R499

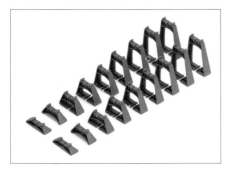

Figure 9.11 Elevated Track Support Set R909

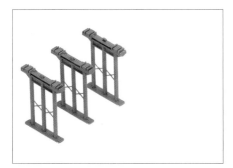

Figure 9.12 High Level Piers R659

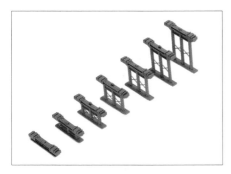

Figure 9.13 Inclined Piers R658

always makes a layout look longer and more exciting to view.

For making up your own tunnels, there is a big selection of separate tunnel mouths available in moulded plastic or card, from several manufacturers and there are also embossed stone sheets by Faller and other makers which have the tunnel mouth shape printed on the back so you can use these card sheets both for retaining walls and for making your own tunnel mouths. Other German firms also make complete tunnel kits. You can also make your own tunnel mouths from card, plastic card, or thin plywood and cover them with brick or stone paper to choice. In card form there are cut-out tunnel mouths from Bilteezi and Metcalfe, which include wing walls, for OO/HO, and repeated in 2mm scale (N) and 3mm scale (TT) by Bilteezi.

If you want tunnel mouths and wing or retaining walls that are strong and realistic, then the Hornby Skaledale range offers them in OO/HO size in stone or brick finish, for single or double track. All butt together well. In some countries (for example the USA) or on narrow gauge lines, tunnel portals may be made of heavy timbers, usually with angled supports, an easy enough scratch-building job.

Bridges and viaducts

Even if your layout is not big enough or hilly enough to need tunnels, you may well need to incorporate bridges or viaducts to cross tracks, canals, rivers, or valleys. A common idea is to use a road overbridge across the tracks to provide the vision break where the track passes from the scenic part of the layout to the fiddle yard or storage tracks behind the scenes. Again there is a very big choice of bridges on the market, many in plastic kit form in all popular scales and depicting all the different types - girder bridge, plate girder bridge, stone bridge, and so on. Sometimes you can combine two kits to make a longer bridge, or conversely shorten a girder bridge by cutting away one or two panels each side. The Skaledale range includes a stone road bridge (R8571) and a brick and plate girder rail bridge (R8570) which are strong enough to be used exactly as they come.

It is worth knowing, too, that some very useful bridges are included in the regular Hornby range, notably a girder bridge with pier supports (R657), a brick overbridge (R189), a viaduct (R180), a river bridge (R499) and a spectacular suspension bridge 1372mm long (R8008). In conjunction with these, Hornby offer sets of inclined piers (R658), elevated track supports (R909) and high level piers (R659), which are useful for taking the track up gradients to fly-over other tracks on the bridges in the range, or for high-level running, etc. These piers support the track, but scenic work is needed to make up embankments to conceal the piers once the track is in place.

Viaducts are more of a special case. There are components in the Skaledale range (R8572, R8612m and R8611) giving piers, walls, and spans to make a viaduct to suit the site by buying enough segments to fit. Some other firms also make viaduct kits or components to allow structures to be built to fit the site, and some curved viaducts are also available. An alternative is to build your own, building the track bed 'flying over' the river or valley, then cladding the structure with card or thin plywood to give the pier and arch shapes, finally covering this work with brick or stone paper. One of the illustrations here shows this being done.

Bridges over rivers, canals, or estuaries can look very attractive on layouts. Ordinary girder, plate, or stone bridges can be used, but in some cases where there was heavy river traffic, rail bridges were required to lift or swing to allow ships through. A few kits

Figure 9.14 A simple wood braced tunnel mouth typical of those on narrow gauge or 'backwoods' lines, made from balsa strip. The locomotive is the Hornby 'Bill' from the 'Thomas' range, converted to 1:32 scale narrow gauge.

Figure 9.15 Road and rail bridges crossing a canal lock on the long-lived Ruxley OO gauge layout of the Epsom & Ewell Model Railway Club. Though built over 45 years ago this club layout is still operating and sets a high standard of planning, detailing, and realism.

Figure 9.16 A bridge across the river on the author's Welney, British HO, layout. The bridge is made from a plastic kit, but note the supporting piers added at each end. The water is depicted by the 'paint and varnish' method as described in Chapter 7.

Figure 9.17 A swing bridge crossing the river on the S gauge layout, East Lynn, built by Trevor Nunn of the British S Scale Society. Everything in the picture is scratch-built in 1:64 scale, but the same idea can be used in other scales.

Figure 9.18 Kits or components for making high viaducts are available from several model firms, including the Hornby Skaledale range. An alternative is to make your own to suit the site. This viaduct is shown under construction on Richard Gardner's big Stokenham OO gauge layout. The wood track bed and supports are being clad with embossed stone sheet at this stage. Note also the valley sides being built, and the impressive backscene painted by Richard Gardner, a skilled artist.

Figure 9.19 The Skaledale double track stone tunnel portal (R8511) in use, with a higher level line routed above it. All other structures here are Skaledale.

Figure 9.20 A Skaledale single track stone tunnel portal (R8509) used here for a road tunnelling under the hill beyond the level crossing. A nicely detailed road bridge crosses the river on the right in this very realistic scene.

Figure 9.19 The Skaledale railway bridge (R8570) shown in use taking the railway over a road on a Hornby demonstration layout. The Hornby Royal Train model is passing through.

have been produced of lift or bascule bridges, though they are non-working, of course, and the rail track is installed across them in the usual way. Same applies to swing bridges. There have been kits for these, too, but it is simple enough to use a suitable girder bridge kit and add the necessary dummy pivots and controls, an example being shown in **Figure 9.17**.

One last item in this chapter is the avalanche tunnel, a structure only found in mountainous areas where a rail route runs below the mountain tops. In some steep spots avalanches of snow, rock, or scree may be encountered, and to protect track and trains from this potential danger a slope-roofed cover is built out over the track. This may be of concrete or heavily braced steel. A few were built in Britain, a notable example being on the Cambrian Coast Line. They are more common in Alpine countries (eg, Switzerland) and make attractive models if your layout setting justifies it.

Chapter Ten

Buildings and details

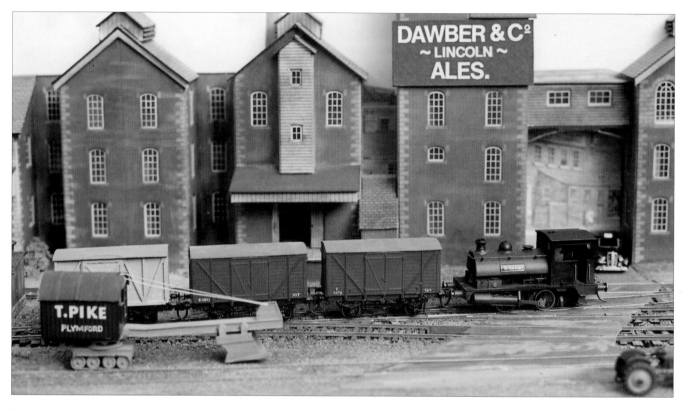

Figure 10.1 Buildings can be the dominant scenery on a small layout. John Pell's HO British industrial layout, with a Hornby Pug converted to a private industry loco, is flanked by factories, warehouses, and this large brewery made from Metcalfe card kits.

Though model structures are generally considered a subject on their own - and there are several very good books on modelling buildings, houses, stations, freight depots and so on, they are as much a part of the scenery as trees, grass, and the landscape in general. In addition to this there are road vehicles, street furniture, telegraph poles, yard lamps, fences and other details that have to find a place in any scenic setting, so you have certainly not completed the scenic work when you finish modelling the last tree, river, or field.

Structures

You can't escape the need for key structures even on the simplest and smallest of layouts. Indeed on the smallest possible shunting layouts the adjacent buildings may form the bulk of the scenic section. For example on the excellent metre-long OO gauge

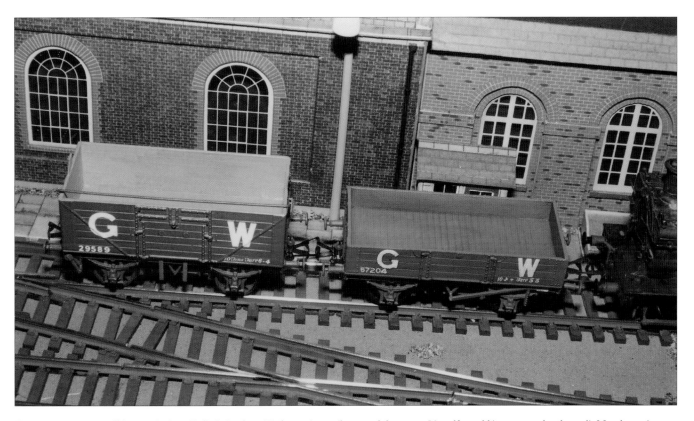

Figure 10.2 A very small layout, Graham Weller's Eastham Works, set in a railway workshop, uses Metcalfe card kits converted to low relief for the entire setting. Wagons are shunted in and out for repair and repainting, allowing plenty of variety.

shunting layout, Eastham Works, made by Graham Weller, which has been seen at some model shows, the setting is within a locomotive and wagon works and the entire short baseboard is backed by red-brick industrial workshops with portals through which the track runs. There is not a hill or tree in sight and the only vegetation modelled is a few weeds alongside the track!

Most layouts, however, have landscape scenery with buildings, too, though as we have seen on a small narrow shelf type layout (some examples are illustrated throughout this book) most of the landscape may actu-ally be on the backscene with just a few bits of embankment, hedge, trees, or foreground areas actually modelled in full. In the chapter on backscenes, building 'flats' were also mentioned and discussed. These are just flat front-ages featured in or glued on to back-scenes. You can make your own, as was described from card, old advert or greeting card illustrations, walls from kits, or your own designs drawn out on card. In addition several firms actually make buildings in scenic flat form as previously noted.

Moving on to fully modelled structures the choice here is immense in the popular OO/HO and N scales, but even larger scales such as O gauge are quite well served. There are numerous ranges of kits, mostly in conventional plastic, and even the Hornby range includes a few of these, such as a restaurant, houses, and some useful electricity pylons, hard to find elsewhere. Kit-built structures are straightforward to build, can be altered a little if you have good modelling experience, and generally cater for all the requirements you are ever likely to have.

There are some wood kits, too, but these need more skill and time to build and as 'craft' items tend to be more expensive. Finally there are plenty of card kits. These in turn can be either of the cut-out variety - by Bilteezi, MZZ (Germany), Auhagen (Germany), Street Level Models, Prototype Models and others - or die-cut type by Superquick, Metcalfe, and others. The latter are on thicker card with press-out components, and make up much more rigidly.

Figure 10.3 On his Lazy River American HO layout, Giles Barnabe made imaginative use of parts from an assortment of left-overs from old plastic kits to make this typical row of old warehouses served by rail. The loading bank is made from balsa.

Figure 10.4 On a compact small East German HO layout built by the author the entire background was made from a MZZ town or city backscene, and the station is from a German kit cut in half and used in low relief. The building at the right is a scenic flat from Bilteezi card parts. Ground level platforms are from balsa sheet, and trees, fence, lamps, telegraph poles and grass are the only other scenic additions.

Despite anything to the contrary that may be given in the instructions for card kits, I find it best to use balsa sheet at least 3mm thick as a backing for all walls on a card cut-out building. I don't bother with the folding tabs along the edges of walls, etc, but simply cut them away. With all the main walls and the roof sections glued to balsa sheet, the walls and roof are cemented together as you might glue up a box or cube. Then to ensure all stays square and never warps, I glue square section balsa strip or stripwood along each inner corner or join, and put bracing strips along longer walls. Use white PVA to glue the cut-out sections to the balsa sheet, and a roller to eliminate any air bubbles. The die-cut models are of thicker cardboard, but I still use square section wood strips, and bracing as required, but rarely balsa sheet on these models. If you omit to do any of this bracing work, card models can all too easily warp in heat and sunlight, or in a damp climate. For the same reason I brace most scenic flat buildings, as noted in Chapter 5.

Plastic building kits rarely offer any constructional problems, but they do need care in assembling and detailing. For example plastic cement (or liquid cement) should be applied with care to stop it oozing out on to the wall

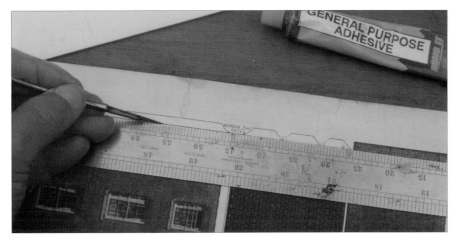

Figure 10.5 Cutting out walls from a Bilteezi card model using a knife and steel rule. Note that the folding tabs are being cut away as the walls will be backed by balsa sheet.

Figure 10.6 Rear view of a card model warehouse converted to low relief and braced inside with wood. The doors have been opened up and dummy floors added from card, with workmen handling cargo.

Figure 10.7 Adding curtains in the windows of a Skaledale builing, then black paper behind some windows to prevent light showing through the structure.

Figure 10.8 The same model, a post office, with curtains added in upper windows, low front windows frosted, and various notices and adverts added.

Figure 10.9 Adding typical 1950s era posters to a Skaledale grocery store. Curtains are also added in the upper windows.

Figure 10.10 The Skaledale corner grocery store with customers and detail added inside, more 1950s adverts and Hornby figures outside, and notices in the windows.

surfaces and spoiling the detail. Doors or windows can often be modelled open or partly open by a small amount of cutting and re-arranging even if no provision is made for this in the kit. Some older kits lack window glazing, so add it yourself from your own spare stock. Most plastic kit buildings these days are pre-coloured, some of them also with weathering. However, some have glossy plastic finish which needs a matt clear varnish coating, and you can depict realistic mortar courses between brickwork by brushing thinned acrylic matt white paint all over a wall section, then wiping it away immediately afterwards, leaving only the white between the bricks. On models with white or buff bricks, use dark grey paint instead.

The most recent trend is for production of fully made up well-detailed finished models. There are several ranges available, a major name being Hornby Skaledale whose models are to OO/HO scale. Most of the models are also reproduced in the Lyddle End range to N scale. In addition there is the Hornby International Skale Structures range. This offers models based on French, German, Italian, and Spanish style prototypes, whereas the Skaledale and Lyddle End ranges are of British prototypes. Nonetheless

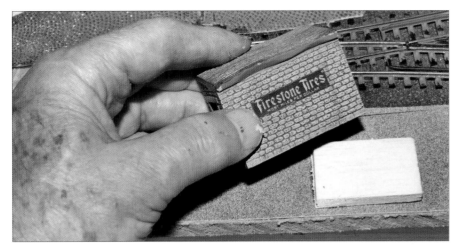

Figure 10.11 This Skaledale store-shed is located close to the baseboard edge and is made removable, fitting over a balsa wood block, so that it can be taken off when the layout is not in use.

Figure 10.12 All the elements of fine scenic work necessary to create a realistic setting can be seen on the superb large Dewsbury Midland OO gauge layout of Manchester Model Railway Society. Here we see a hand-painted backscene, a factory as a scenic flat, a tall low relief warehouse (right) and fully modelled terraced houses (foreground), all accurately reflecting the Dewsbury area.

Figure 10.13 The SkaleLighting system allows buildings to be lit up for night effects, as shown in this Skaledale signal box which has also had figures and interior details added.

Figure 10.14 On the author's O scale narrow gauge American layout, Western Landing, the station (centre) and freight shed (left) were scratch-built from wood in low relief to fit the space between track and backscene. The store just visible at right is converted from a plastic toy item.

Figure 10.15 On the Snailspeed Light Railway layout of Brian Taylor, in OO gauge, most of the structures are scratch-built in wood or card. This is the locomotive depot, packed with nice detail. Equally good is the scenic treatment behind, with distant trees painted on the background.

Figure 10.16 Spare walls and roofs left over from other kits were used to make this small local brewery on the author's German HO St Kathrein layout. The tall water tanks are sweetener tubes painted silver-grey.

there is some potential for cross-border changes. I changed a Skaledale British station building, for example, into a convincing looking German one simply by adding German nameboards, German adverts, and a German style clock. Conversely some of the Skale Structures models, such as the goods shed and rural shed could pass for British. Realism is good throughout.

All these models are moulded in a hard resin material, hollow inside, but there are new models coming out all the time, often replacing earlier ones of the same type, and you need to refer to the current catalogues to see what is available or due soon.

In addition to the structures themselves there is an ever-growing range of accessories including road signs old and new, street lamps, dustbins, skips, wagon loads of several types, milk churns, post boxes and much more. Numerous other companies, of course, also offer accessories such as yard lamps, telegraph poles, fencing, cargoes, sign posts and so on.

Most buildings would normally be glued down or otherwise affixed to the baseboard, but some modellers prefer to make large or vulnerable structures removable. You might do this, for example on a portable layout, or a large layout that may be taken to

model shows. Key structures can be kept safely boxed when the layout is not actually in use. The normal method of doing this is to fix a balsa block, 1in (24cm) or more deep, in position on the layout over which the building can be fitted and held snugly in place.

Low relief

At this point it is worth covering the useful idea of low relief structures (sometimes called half relief), the idea here being taken from what is done on theatre stages or film sets - in other words only the visible front section of a structure is modelled, thus saving a great deal of depth. On a small layout this may be a necessity if, say, your shelf-type baseboard is only 9 inches wide. Tracks may take up 6 inches of this width leaving only 3 inches or so for buildings. So long as these are behind the track you can depict all required structures in low relief. Combined with a good background they can look very convincing. Some of the modern resin models have been produced in low relief, such as the Skaledale terraced houses and one or two small shops, and some card or die-cut card models are specifically produced for low relief.

But aside from these you can make your own low relief models by cutting

Figure 10.17 A card cut-out low relief warehouse from the Auhagen/Sipp range being glued to the 'sky' backscene. It is being positioned to obscure the join in the backscene boards, visible on the right.

down full depth kits, using just the front 1-2 inches (25-50cm) as desired. There is a 'bonus' to this idea, for the unused sections of the kit can be kept and used elsewhere for other low relief structures.

Finally, if you have the skills low relief models can be scratch-built to suit the site or space available if nothing else will fit.

Detailing structures

Both plastic kit structure models and resin ready-made models of the Skaledale type can be enhanced or given extra character by adding some details. Obviously the degree of detailing you do will vary with the building and its function. It can also vary with the amount of work you want to put in. For example you could put floors into multi-storey buildings by cutting out balsa or card inserts and cementing them in place. Same applies to internal walls. However, bear in mind that in OO or HO scale the structures are still quite small and you can't see far into the buildings anyway, so some intricate interior detail can be added, as I've discovered in the past, only for it to be hardly visible when the model is viewed from eye-level.

The most important task, I've found, is to stop light being visible right

Figure 10.18 Two views of the same 4mm scale farm show the standard of detailing to aim for. Points to note are the realistic cows being taken in for milking, the stack of churns, perfectly weathered buildings, lichen on barn roof, rough farmyard ground, field and tree, and the hand-made fence.

Figure 10.19 Excellent modelling on a harbour layout with a well-weathered Hornby GWR pannier tank shunting wagons on the stone-faced jetty and a realistic row of warehouses behind. Note crew in the loco cab, the 'cameo' of a boy on a bicycle, and a quayside crane.

through the building, which is the most obvious give-away that the structure is just a hollow shell. The simple answer here is to black out all the windows and add curtains to suit. This gives a nice 'lived in' look and stops any chance of light shining through the building. You can do this using coloured paper for curtains, and backing them with black paper rectangles, all glued carefully behind the windows. Tweezers aid positioning. If you've got any left-over printed curtains/black-outs from Faller or Kibri kits, etc, you can use them instead of cutting out your own.

For a 'frosted' glass effect, as on bath-room windows, use white or off-white thin paper glued inside.

There is a great deal that can be done in the way of extra detailing. This includes adding suitable figures in shops, visible counters and stock in shops, cycle racks outside, trestle tables with extra stock outside shops, adverts on walls, adverts in shop windows. Seats can be added in waiting rooms (as can passengers), workers inside factories, and so on. You are only limited here by your imagination - and observation of the real thing - and the

work can be absorbing especially if you are adding levers and controls inside a signal box!

Linked with structure work is the clever and compact Hornby SkaleLighting system that enables buildings to be lit up realistically for night scenes, though not all modellers go this far. If you do go for it everything is fairly straightfor-ward on the 'plug and play' principle, but you need to paint the interiors of all buildings, resin or plastic, in matt black to prevent any 'glow' through the walls. Some plastic kits supply black paper cut-outs to suit the insides of the

Figure 10.20 A BR Class 121 Driving Motor Brake approaching the station.

Figure 10.21 Good realism can be achieved even in a very small space, as this view of a J94 0-6-0ST shunting a short siding shows. The coal staithes here are from the Skaledale range.

walls, again for use if interior lighting is added.

Road vehicles

Just like buildings, road vehicles are also part of the scenery, so they need similar attention. All too often layouts display glossy models of cars, trucks, or buses devoid of drivers, passengers, and often cargo in the case of trucks. True, parked cars and trucks will not have drivers, but on the road they do. Most plastic road vehicles can be dis-assembled fairly easily to enable figures to be inserted and there are sets of seated people available. Recent die-cast vehicles tend to be screw-assembled, so they can also be taken apart and re-assembled after suitable figures have been put in.

Few road vehicles get really dirty, but they are rarely as glossy as new models, so it is a good idea to give each new road vehicle you get a coat of matt clear varnish. A little greyish-brown round the tyre treads helps, and on some models it is possible to bend the front axle slightly so that a parked vehicle has a bit of lock on its wheels, as is often seen in real life.

Cameos

Also part of every day scenery is some of the activity that helps trade proceed.

Figure 10.22 A complete small town gas works of the 1950s is an attractive scenic feature possible with Skaledale (OO), or Lyddle End (N) models.

Figure 10.23 A superb farm setting from Skaledale models, with wooded background from Skale Scenics, on a Hornby demonstration layout by Nevile Reid.

Figure 10.24 A marshalling yard with double engine goods shed.

For example cargo being loaded into a truck, cargo being unloaded from a box van, forklift trucks at work, and so on. Also there is activity on farms or at factories. These are usually called cameo scenes and can add a lot of interest and charm to any layout. Some humorous scenes are favoured by some modellers, such as the bus held up by a flock of sheep, or a long bus queue.

What ever you do, it is certainly good to concentrate on activity at stations or in warehouses, freight depots, docksides, etc, for this suggests your railway has a purpose - moving cargoes and passengers. Without some evidence of this a layout can look very dull. There is no shortage of model figures in OO/HO and the smaller and larger scales. Preiser and Noch have big ranges and

the Hornby range includes several sets of key figures including workers and seated passengers for OO/HO size. Because figures are 'frozen' in position, many modellers prefer to use figures in fairly static poses, though it is largely a matter of choice. If you want a football match depicted, or people running for the train, you can please yourself on this.

Figure 10.25 Bartellos' Big Top Circus with in the foreground three vehicles from the Skale Autos range which all add authenticity to a layout.

Chapter Eleven

Practical projects

Practical Projects

As noted in the opening chapter of this book, there is rather more to scenic modelling than just the obvious subjects of backgrounds, hills, trees, and vegetation. You are trying to create a complete picture of a world in miniature so this involves all sorts of detail work, structures, road vehicles, and even figures as part of the scene. In the final section of the book, here are a few practical projects to give some idea of what can be done to give your own model rail world an extra degree of character and detail.

Road vehicles

In the previous chapter I remarked that road vehicles and, indeed, cameo scenes of activity in detail are all part of the model world that reflects real life. Many modellers buy car, truck, or bus models and place them on the layout straight out of the box. Thus we see cars running down the street with no driver on board, and even more obviously model buses are seen with no crew or passengers, while trucks carry no loads unless one is included with the model as purchased. All these shortcomings can be remedied. Model

Figure 1 The Hornby Skale Auto Land Rover has a screw assembly and can be taken apart so that the seats can be painted and driver added.

Figure 2 When re-assembled the driver adds a nice touch and avoids the common layout sight of driverless cars waiting at level-crossings.

Figure 3 Very basic detailing added to Roco HO German Magirus rental truck. The front axle has been bent to put some 'parking lots' on the wheels. The wheel treads are weathered, tail lights are painted red, and licence plates are front and rear.

road vehicles is almost a model subject in its own right, but the illustrations here give some key examples of what can be done to make models more realistic, and as with model trains a certain amount of weathering can be added, too, particularly on wheels to make the model look as though it has actually run up some mileage.

Model road vehicles are widely available in the popular model railway scales – including 1,0,00,HO, and N and the work is similar in all scales though only 00 and HO are shown here. Ready-made models come in die-cast form (including the Hornby Skale Auto range), and many more come in plastic. There are also a few assembly kits in metal or plastic. To keep the subject to a reasonable length here is a summary of the main work need to make model road vehicles even more realistic.

■ Look out for modern metal models which are screw-assembled. They take apart easily for internal detailing. **See Figure A.1.**

■ Most plastic model road vehicles can be taken apart also for internal painting and detailing, and for fitting of drivers and passengers, etc.

■ Check model for licence plates or

Figure 4 Buses are often seen on layouts empty of crew or passenger – not even a driver. This SES plastic HO East german IFA bus (of Meissner City Transport) has been dis-assembled, interior painted, driver and two passengers added, and luggage glued on the roof rack (which is accessed by a rear ladder). Wheelhubs and front and rear lights were also painted in, and licence plates added.

Figure 5 Delivery trucks with tail-lifts have been common in the past 30 years or so, but they are rarely modelled. It is an easy enough job to add one from scratch as on this Mercedes van – upright.

number plates. Some have them as purchased, otherwise be sure to add them. Also check rear and turn light details. Sometimes you need to paint them in.

■ Similarly check other details which may need to be added, such as rear-view mirrors, screen wipers. Some

models have them, others don't, and with some models they come as add-on parts.

■ Light weathering (don't overdo it) can give a model a 'used' look. At least weather the wheels or tyre treads, etc. Some models can be given an old well weathered look simply by carefully

Figure 6 Fork-lift trucks can be enhanced by adding a driver figure, plus a pallet with a typical load. This model for HO has also had the wheel hubs painted.

Figure 7 Driver figure, licence plates, and rear-view mirrors have been added to this vintage 1929 Mercedes lorry. The cab was unclipped from the chassis to get the driver inside.

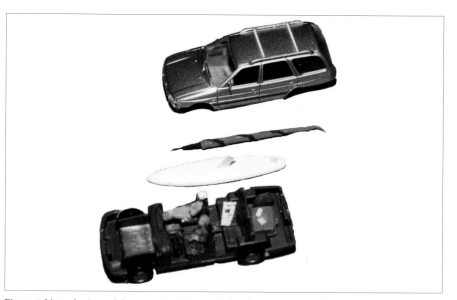

Figure 8 Most plastic model cars can be disassembled easily for extra detailing. Here a passenger and driver have been added, plus a newspaper on the back seat and a suitcase (with labels) in rear luggage space. A sailboard and furled mast/sail have been made to glue on the roof-rack. Number plates are also added.

Figure 9 This HO scale Iveco articulated truck has been repainted in matt colours, had company markings added, and here rear-view mirrors (from black card) are being glued in place. Also added are number plates and screen wipers.

Figure 10 The Iveco articulated truck model after completion, with light weathering on the lower body sides. Behind is an American truck given similar treatment.

painting them with matt clear varnish, especially those with a high gloss finish as purchased. This particularly applies to commercial vehicles.

■ Many modern trucks and vans, etc. have tail-lifts. You can add them by simple scratch-built additions (see above), either in 'operating' mode, or in the folded up position. A dummy tail-lift allows cameo scenes, as on p121, to be set up at warehouses and freight depots.

■ Add dummy cargo items in open trucks or pick-ups, preferably ones you can remove. Some models come with cargo, others don't. Many trucks even when running 'light' carry a folded tarpaulin in the load space. A quick way to depict this is with folded tissue paper, glued inside the folds, and painted matt dark grey, and glued on the flatbed of the cargo space. A tarpaulin over the load in a truck (or railway wagon) can be made from thin tissue (the tissue paper of a teabag is best) laid over the load and painted over with matt clear varnish. This will make the tissue 'droop' realistically over the load. When the varnish is dry, paint the tarpaulin dark grey.

Figure 11 'Cameo' scenes can add much interest to any layout, and a good example is this gang of track workers with their pick-up truck on the Canadian Glendale layout of Roger Nicholls. Note also other small details like the switchgear cabinet (left), and dustbin and old pallets (right). Photo by Tony Morris.

Figure 12 Considerable work is needed to make convincing road scenes. Here is a dual carriageway modelled with a tram track in the centre, zebra crossing, street lamps, weathered road surfaces, well placed figures, and a detailed shop window display.

A Light Railway Station

When a cricket pavilion was introduced in the Hornby Skaledale range, quite a few modellers realised that it quite closely resembled a light railway station of the sort found on the lines run by Colonel Stephens, and it was evident that the potential for conversion was good. The photographs here show how to do it, though, there are other options. For example this conversion has a ground level platform, but it could equally well be built on a more conventional high platform, simply by using thick balsa sheet rather than the thin sheeting used here.

While the pavilion is not an exact look-alike to any light railway station that the author could find in any photographs, the approximate size and style is similar, notably the frontage, the wood construction, and the canopy. Most of the Colonel Stephens stations of this sort, for example, on the KESR had a lean-to store shed at one end and a primitive 'gents' at the other. These are added to the model here but, again, they are options and could be omitted or made in a different style – take your pick of these variations. You end up with a delightful little light railway station of character.

Figure 1 The cricket club lettering was painted out and replaced with a station name, and PLR – Pillsburgh Light Railway – at the ends of the nameboard. Note the added timetable and advert.

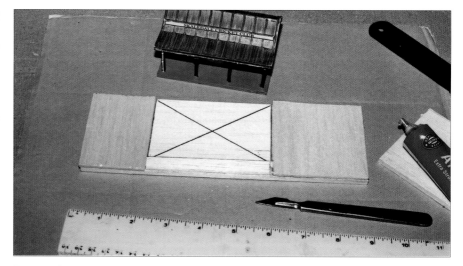

Figure 2 The ground level platform is made from two 5mm thick sheets of balsa with a gap left (diagonal cross) to recess the pavilion base. The platform measures 9ins x 3ins (227mm x 75mm).

Figure 3 Faller embossed brick is used to to finish off the platform edges, but embossed stone or other makes of brick paper are options.

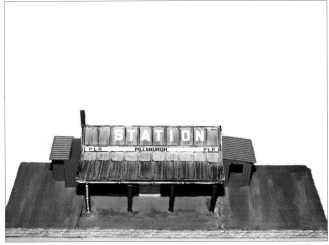

Figure 4 Station glued into platform recess with 'gents' on the left and store shed on the right added at each end from corrugated card.

Figure 5 The Skaledale cricket pavilion after conversion to light railway station. Gas lamps, seat, churns are also Skaledale.

Figure 6 The 4 wheel coach has end steps, necessary for access to the ground level platform. It has been disassembled to add passengers.

An Oil Storage Tank

Some freight facilities served by rail on real railways are very large, so we tend to choose smaller types for layouts where space is limited. An oil refinery or fuel distribution depot would be too big to depict on most layouts but a small oil storage tank is a neat facility you can fit into any layout, but its small size and compactness makes it specifically suited to small layouts. On a shelf-type layout a narrow 'footprint' is especially useful as quite a lot of kit-built or ready-made structures are too wide to fit on. This little model, as made here, is only 38mm wide in OO/HO size which means it can be tucked in almost anywhere. Most oil depots cover quite a big area but this small oil storage tank gives good visual justification for running tank wagons on your layout even if you haven't got room for a bigger oil facility.

An oil storage tank, too, can be used in conjunction with other facilities. Aside from acting as a storage for a local fuel merchant in a country goods yard, it could be found in a harbour setting with the fuel supply for fishing boats, and in earlier days they could be seen holding oil supplies for industrial plants or small local power stations.

Though most of these oil storage tanks had a similar layout, they could

Figure 1 Components of the model: cradles from 10mm thick balsa with (in this case) 13mm radius cut outs to take the tank from an old American tank car.

vary a good deal in construction and detail. Quite a few oil storage tanks used old tanks taken from scrapped tank wagons and this was what was used for the model shown here. It came from a 'junked' American tank car in a battered state bought for a few pence at a model show bric-a-brac stall. However, any other tube shape of similar size could be used, or the tank from any other long tank wagon. The cradles were made from 10mm thick balsa sheet cut to 35mm wide and 60mm high. Cut-outs to take the tank were carved out to 13mm radius at each cradle top, using a sharp new blade in the craft knife. Obviously this

cut-out can be sized to match whatever you use for a tank. At the base of each cradle a 2mm square balsa strip was glued to suggest sunken foundations for each cradle. The useful Skaledale 'rear extension' (R869) is a perfect pump house. The cradles were first painted 'concrete' colour and lightly weathered with a few rain streaks. Then they were glued at each end of the pump house, the tank was glued in the cradles, and that was all the hard work done.

Extra work was done to add a ladder each side up to the platform flanking the dome on the tank. If you use a different tank without a centre dome an option is to glue a catwalk on top of the tank with an access ladder at one end. Finally a discharge pipe for tank wagons, with an operating wheel, was glued on the track side of the pump house, and the final task is to add warning signs each side of the pump house, a notice on the pump house front, and some trade adverts, though these are optional. If you model any time before about 1965, there are plenty of old-time oil trade adverts and signs in Tiny signs packs 63 (00) and 69 (N), and others.

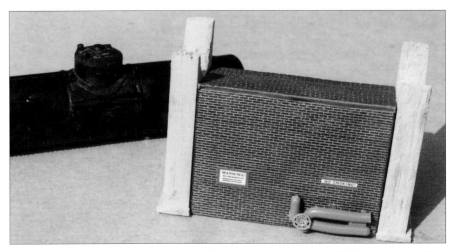

Figure 2 Model from the rear with cradels glued to hut, tank ready to fit, and discharge pipes made from scrap plastic sprue.

Figure 3 Rear view of the model showing warning signs, ladder, pipes and control wheel (from scrap items) supposedly for pumping oil from wagons.

Figure 4 Skaledale 'rear extension' balsa cradles painted as concrete, and ladder to the centre platform on the tank.

Unloading a wagon

Though there are plenty of model figures available to populate model railway layouts, only in rare instances have they been animated so that they appear to move. Lack of movement of figures doesn't really worry anyone but it is always worth positioning figures in key places where you might expect to see a person in real life.

The most obvious example is the locomotive crew. On all my model loco-motives, I add crew figures to the cab if they are not already placed there by the manufacturers. Yet how many layouts do you see, especially at model shows, where there is nobody in the cab? In similar fashion, I add a few passengers in coaches and a guard in the guard's van, all simple but pleasing tasks for hobbyists.

One thing I recall vividly from my youth is seeing men using shovels to empty coal out of coal wagons at local coaling stages or, more often, in the coal merchant's siding at my local station. But again, on layouts it is rare to see this activity depicted.

Wagons are shunted mostly into a siding, then hauled out again later with no visual indication that any coal has been unloaded. There is a limitation, it is true, in that it would look equally

Figure 1 The 'dummy' wagon with men inside uploading it. It never moves from the siding. Note the coal on the ground below the open door and another man in the coal yard plus, in this case, a coal conveyor made from a length of wide plastic girder on a chassis made from scrap plastic. The wagon is weathered and dirtied (with coal dust and rust) by careful brush painting. The figures are from the Dapol railway worker set.

unlikely for wagons to be hauled around the layouts in a goods train with the men standing inside them,

So what is the answer? How can we suggest that coal really is unloading in the siding? Well, the way to do it is by using a 'dummy' wagon, up near the buffers in the siding, that stays there always. In it two men are positioned shovelling out the coal and the wagon has only part of its coal left inside.

Coal is depicted spilled on the track-side below the open door, too. What happens is that other coal wagons are shunted in and out of the siding in the usual way but that wagon stays there. It seems to create a good illusion.

At shows, I hear viewers saying 'Look, they are actually unloading the coal on this layout'. They don't really notice that the wagon concerned is always there. The suggestion of activity is good enough.

The model shown is actually made from the Dapol kit of a 16 ton BR wagon because the kit has an opening door which makes the project easy. But you can use any other coal wagon, including Hornby and side door can be cut out with a razor-saw and glued in the open position.

If you happen to have an old wagon which is no longer a good runner, maybe with a wobbly wheel, using it as a 'dummy' will allow it to continue giving good service.

This same trick can be used with other open flat wagons, for example with a load of planks or bagged fertiliser. Arrange your figures to be handling the load and position the wagon up against the buffer stops. All other wagons can be stopped short of it. This is a very good example of a 'cameo scene' as suggested elsewhere in this book.

Figure 2 A coaling tower from the Hornby Skaledale range.

Agricultural warehouse from the Skaledale Mill

The Skaledale range of structures from Hornby are good, not least because they are hollow with 'see through' windows and have excellent texture and colouring as they come. This makes them truly ready to use with no further work needed.

You can utilise some of the Skaledale country buildings for rail-related use, however, and the one that caught my eye was the Hubbards Hill Water Mill (R8508). This model reminded me of the sort of buildings that could be seen years ago on country branch lines. The notable feature is the hoist and doorway to the upper storey which is visually attractive. On these country lines you could see a siding serving agricultural warehouses. Some of these were farmers' co-ops where farmers brought seasonal produce by truck, wagon or tractor for shipping out by rail and sometimes for pre-packing into boxes or sacks too. Other structures house 'feed and see' merchants bringing in seeds, fertilisers, animal foods and even machinery for supply to local farmers. Sometimes these roles were combined in one company and in one building.

You could use the Hubbards's Mill

model as it comes and simply make a card or balsa lean-to-extension to cover the waterwheel. I made a store room section with loading bank, which gave it a nice balanced frontage 19cms long which can accommodate an equally nice long siding set in front.

I made the store room extension and loading bank fom odd walls and roof sections left over from other kit conversions in the past. If you have also made kit buildings you may have similar oddments which can be used in the same way. The alternative is to make a similar extension entirely from card or balsa wood or a combination of the two. For those of you who choose this option, I have included an outline drawing of the structure I made, see figure 5. You do not have to duplicate my dimensions exactly – you can have higher walls and a longer extension if you wish, depending on the space available.

A further alternative, if you prefer to use kit parts, is to get the Wills country barn kit and use the front wall, roof and half-width ends from that kit. You do not need to make a deep model since this structure will only be seen from the front – if you locate it behind a siding.

On the Hubbard Hill Mill itself, I added a 24mm (high) by 20mm double

door from card over the lower front window bay and from balsa I made the small folding platform (glued in the 'up' position) that is usually seen on warehouse floors with hoists. I also added the hoist rope to the gantry over the upper floor by cementing brown cotton round it. Wagons of, say, fertiliser in bags, would be positioned under the hoist so that the load could be hauled up to the upper level for storage.

Bear in mind that some Skaledale structures are replaced from time to time with different but similar ones. You could use any other similar size and shape building if you can't find the mill.

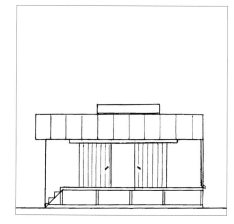

Figure 5 Drawing of side extension – double the dimensions for the model.

Figure 1 The Skaledale Hubbards Mill model as it comes.

Figure 2 Building the extension using spare wall and roof sections and loading bank from a plastic kit walkway glued on a balsa strip. Dummy sliding doors for the storage section are cut from card (seen in the foreground). The lower storey window is covered by a card double door and a folding platform is glued below the upper storey door.

Figure 3 Painting is completed and the side extension is glued to the mill to conceal the water wheel. A balsa strip covers the roof gap.

Figure 4 Added nameboard and advert, plus drainpipes, complete the model.

A warehouse siding

An interesting feature of many goods yards in earlier days was a siding serving warehouses belonging to local firms who shipped in or despatched products by rail.

Some big yards had several sidings like this. Typical businesses with these warehouses might deal in wood, foods, building material, furniture, white goods and much more. Freight forwarders might also operate from here. In Britain, this sort of operation has largely disappeared except for a few large freight terminals but they can still be seen in other countries such as Germany or USA.

On a recent layout in N scale, I incorporated a warehouse siding at the back of the goods yard. Here there was no room for full depth structures in front of the backscene, to all the warehouses were depicted as scenic flats instead. Other structures on the layout were from Lyddle End models and you can mix full depth models and scenic flats on the same layout quite effectively.

The easy way to make scenic flat buildings is to adapt suitable walls and frontages from card cutout buildings which are widely available in N and 00/HO scales – in most cases the same building is reproduced in both scales.

Figure 1 A freight forwarder frontage was made from one side of a kit warehouse, with the frontage glued to a 5mm thick balsa sheet. A strip of balsa with the end sawn off to form a ramp was used as a loading bank. The roof was another strip of thin balsa wood.

You can buy these from larger model shops and they are often sold at large model railways shows too.

The models can be built to full-depth but they are very adaptable to suit any requirements and the photographs of the scenic flats on my layout show how it can be done. You can, of course, adapt any of the card kits available to suit your needs. It is also possible to make your own card warehouse frontages and an example is included here.

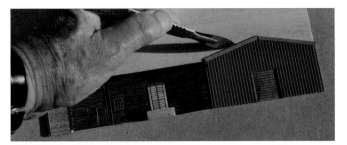

Figure 2 A wood warehouse was made from the side and one end of a card goods shed sheet.

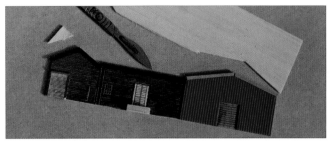

Figure 3 Here are the two warehouses cut out and ready to fix in place.

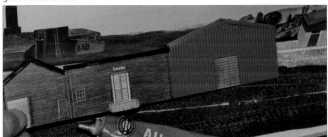

Figure 4 The two warehouses here and the freight forwarder – are glued to the backscene board behind the warehouse siding.

Figure 5 Before the warehouses were affixed, a paved area was glued alongside the siding using paving strips, also seen here.

Figure 6 The completed warehouse siding on the layout after additional scenic finishing of the ground area. The German DB class 0-6-0T shunting loco and the wagons are form the Hornby International Arnold N scale range.

An elevated signal box

We normally see signal boxes at ground level alongside the track or; at least, we did in the old days of 'traditional' mechanical signal boxes. But there were cases where there was not enough room alongside the tracks for a signal box to be sited and the answer then was usually to raise it to an elevated position straddling the tracks. Sometimes very large signal boxes were positioned like this and elevated signal boxes carrying many levers and of great width were once well-known on the approaches to major stations, such as Clapham Junction and Waterloo.

However, there are plenty of examples of smaller elevated versions. One was at Hexham on the Newcastle–Carlisle line looking very much like the model made here, except that the four major uprights were clad in brickwork rather than being just bare girders. You could see elevated signal boxes even on branch lines.

A prime example was at Perranwell on the GWR Falmouth branch. Here the station was in a right cutting and the signal box straddled the bay siding. It was actually smaller than the model, on the width of the small box itself, but with a similar girder support.

When the Hornby Skaledale models

Figure 1 Here are the parts laid out: support girders from a Dapal bridge, a wood planked platform from Wills accessory sheets cut to 68mm x 55mm spare ladder and fencing and the Skaledale range.

appeared, I found you could use some of them in different ways. The small level crossing signal box is a case in point, for little structures like this could also be seen as signal boxes on branch line platforms and controlling small goods yards. In the Hornby book of Model Railways the author made a small narrow goods yard layout called Westwood sidings.

As it was only 6 inches wide, I faced the same problem as a real railway yard would on a narrow site. The only place to put the signal box controlling the yard and its approaches was in an elevated position at the entrance to the yard. The Skaledale level crossing box is just the right size, and you can make a simple elevated platform for it to stand on. You will need to use some girder panels from a girder bridge kit and some fencing strips. The critical dimensions to span a single track and clear the trains running underneath are 72mm wide across the supports and a floor height of 64mm.

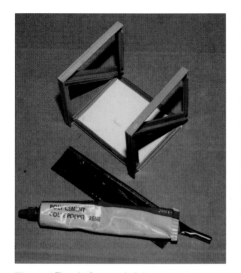

Figure 2 The platform and girder supports are glued together on a flat surface to ensure they set completely square.

Figure 3 The side fences and the ladder are glued in place and left overnight to set.

Figure 4 The signal box can now be fitted. Note that a signalmen figure has been glued in the doorway.

Figure 5 The model completed and painted, with some weathering on the girders.

Figure 6 The elevated signal box glued in place. Note that some foliage is added growing round the bottom of the girders and a yard lamp has been glued to one of the girder uprights.

An end loading ramp

In the days, not so long ago, when more general freight was moved by rail, such as parcels, milk churns, barrels and created goods were commonly loaded or unloaded from platforms or loading banks at goods depots. These were side loaded through doors of box vans or open wagons.

However, wheeled vehicles such as cars, tractors, lorries, trailers and farm machinery were more easily loaded or unloaded by wheeling them on and off the wagons over the ends. To do this, an end-on platform or ramp was needed.

These end loading ramps actually varied quite a lot. In big freight yards, they might be built into the end of a loading bank to give an end and side loading facility on the same siding. In smaller yards, there was often a separate end loading ramp at the end of a siding instead of a buffer stop. A flat wagon or Lowmac carrying a wheeled vehicle was simply shunted up to the ramp and the yard workers pushed – or even drove – the vehicle off the wagon and down the slope to the ground.

End loading ramps could be made of brick and concrete like a station platform but there were also some made of steel and quite a few made of wood.

Figure 1

Figure 2

The latter type is very easy to model and it makes a nice addition to any goods yard, well suited to a branch line setting. As it happens, there are few – if any – end loading ramps available ready-made, so making your own is the way to get one.

■ Figure 1 Packs of assorted balsa sheet and strips are sold in many model shops – useful for many modelling needs. For the loading ramp, you need a sheet of 3mm balsa wood. Use a ruler and ballpoint pen to draw out the ramp decking, 48mm wide, with a front (horizontal) section 20mm long and the sloped ramp 60mm long. The craft knife blade here points to the 20mm section. Draw in parallel lines at 5mm spacing to depict the heavy timbers used on the ramp. Use of the ballpoint pen for this indents the balsa wood

Figure 3

surface to give a good effect of individual timbers when the model is painted. When the drawing work is finished, use a metal rule and craft knife to cut it out. For the front support, cut a 48mm length from a 12mm square balsa strip with a razor-saw, as shown top right. Always seek an adult's assistance when handling craft knife.

■ Figure 2 The ramp can be assembled in position at the end of the siding, in place of the more usual buffer stop. The front support is set back from the front to allow for the coupler to pass under-

neath. A flat wagon is being used here to check this. Side supports are made from small balsa strips cut to length and glued under the side of the ramp, as shown. Once the assembly is done, leave it overnight for the glue to dry.

■ Figure 3 Use acrylic dark earth paint to colour the balsa ramp, applied quite lightly so that the planking marks show through. A touch of grey was worked in while the paint was still wet. An extra strip bas been added to the baseboard edge here to allow more scenic development. When the paint was dry, some

bushes, grass ballast from the Skale Scenics range were glued around the ramp area to complete the scene. Here a Hornby Lowmac with Skale Autos farm tractor is pushed up to the ramp by a BR Terrier loco, while the yard crew prepare to unload it. Note an extra baulk of timber using balsa strip, placed across the buffers to ensure the tractor wheels don't get stuck in the gap. In the background, a Scammell mechanical horse form the Corgi trackside range passes by.

Making a small halt

Stations can take up a lot of room on a layout, certainly if modelled to anything like scale length. If you have a small layout, such as the short 4 ft long 00 scale harbour layout featured in this book, then a small halt might be a better idea for the passenger service. My halt happens to be a terminus too, since it simply serves the harbour branch but there were real examples of such a setting. Most halts are passing stops but my model as made could be used in any setting.

Follow the photographs to see how to construct it.

■ Figure 1 The platform was cut from the sheet of 8mm thick balsa wood (sold in large model shops) seen in the background. It is 22cm long and 4cm wide – long enough for a diesel railcar to stop – but you can make it longer if you have the space. A ramp was sawn into one end. As an option you can put one at both ends if desired. The balsa sheet was covered with printed paving card from a kit, of which there is quite a variety on the market. You can also make the platform higher if desired but it looks 'longer' if kept low and quite a few halts had low platforms or even ground level platforms. GWR

railcars and auto-trailers, as made by Hornby, had steps built in to allow for low platforms.

■ Figure 2 The platform was glued in place on the layout and spare lengths of the paving card were used for the station approach and parking area. The halt waiting room is R8718 Lower Skaledale Shelter. I added window glazing and filled in the side opening with card panels, one with an advert added and the other a timetable board. Just visible on the side there is added a fire locker for hose etc. that was made from scrap plastic. The edges of the low platform have been painted 'concrete' colour.

■ Figure 3 To fill in the rough ground behind the halt, use R8070 modelling rock, which is 'wetted' and cut into shape.

■ Figure 4 The modelling rock is worked into position with your fingers. Off-cuts of card and balsa (as visible in the foreground) can be used under the modelling rock to give it an uneven 'rough ground' shape.

■ Figure 5 When dry, the modelling rock is painted 'earth' colour. Note that the grass mat has been used on

the area in front of the halt.

■ Figure 6 Scatter material depicting grass and gravel is glued over the painted area and then clumps of foliage are glued in place to depict undergrowth and bushes.

■ Figure 7 To complete the setting, a fence is glued along the back of the platform, a Skaledale bicycle is propped against it and a R8673 station lamp is glued at the rear corner of the shelter to illuminate the platform. Passengers and a parked car complete the scene as the GWR railcar arrives, while a GWR Terrier shunts in the background.

Figure 1

Figure 2

Figure 5

Figure 3

Figure 4

Figure 6

Figure 7

A compact seaport scene

In this modern age, the only seaports that now have a rail connection tend to be those that have a container, oil or LPG terminal. Specialist rail vehicles – container flats and big tank wagons – are used for this traffic.

In the old days, thirty or more years ago, there were many more active ports that handled cargo of all sorts and nearly all of them had rail connections ranging from one or two sidings on a quayside in a very small harbour – such as Minehead in Somerset – to an extremely complex rail system in its own right like the Port of London Authority railways, serving miles of docks and jetties in London – all now disappeared.

On a modern layout, a seaport setting can add a lot of visual interest but it also justifies lots of shunting action using wagons of all types to handle varied cargoes such as timber, crated machinery, bagged fertiliser, oil in drums or almost anything else you can think of.

At Watchet, for instance, esparto grass from Spain was landed for use in the papermaking industry. On a layout, however, even a small seaport modelled in full would take up quite a large area, so a popular way of avoiding this is to model a jetty with just enough room for a small ship at the front of the layout, leaving the rest of the harbour to the viewer's imagination.

An alternative idea is to model most of the seaport on the backscene which can reduce it to just a few millimetres deep while giving the impression of great space and activity. This is what I did on my Berghaven layout, which is only 5ft long and less than 12ins (30cm) wide. I decided to use the back edge of the baseboard as the quayside.

After this the procedure was easier than you might expect. Model shops sell the relevant manufacturers' scenic sheets to achieve busy looking harbour backscenes. You just need to glue your selected scene to a hardboard backboard in the way previously shown.

I chose a medium size harbour scene to glue to the backboard, using a roller to ensure no air bubbles were left to spoil the effect. Another alternative on offer provided me with a nice looking motor coaster on it that looks close to 4mm (00) scale, so I bought that as well, using sharp scissors to cut out the coaster from the scene.

The mast, flagpole etc. were not cut out. I glued the boat to thick card, then cut it out and glued it between the backboard and rear baseboard edge to give the impression of the ship berthed alongside.

When the glue had set, I added mast and derrick from wooden cocktail sticks and used scrap plastic as a bollard on the jetty, with cotton thread as a head-rope securing it.

On the jetty, I glued a Skaledale set of packing cases, depicting cargo being handled. This also concealed some men printed on the ship's side doing some painting. Both the harbour scene and ship were flat and to this I also added a flat crane on the jetty.

The crane was made from a scrap piece of corrugated plastic sheeting, whilst the ladder, roof strip, door and base were all scrap plastic items I had available, which is why all keen modellers should keep oddments left over from kits for later use in projects like this! The jib was part of an old broken crane but could have been made from any plastic strip glued to shape.

The photographs are taken from a a higher angle so the arrangement is clear but when the layout is operated at eye-level, which is my usual way of working, the entire scene looks surprisingly 'deep' and the fact that the crane, ship and warehouses beyond are all flat, is not immediately obvious.

As I've noted before, such model

scenic work can be copied from film, theatre and TV scenic methods where lots of tricks are used to give an impression of depth that is not really there.

Figure 1 BR Class 08 shunting the quayside. Note the driver added in the cab. The wagon load is from Skaledale and the Skale Auto British Rail van has been given a coat of clear matt varnish to tone down the gloss finish.

Figure 2 The finished scene with no trains in the way to obscure it so that the arrangement can be seen. Note headrope on the ship and mast and derrick from wooden cocktail sticks glued in the correct place on the scenery. The grand cover here is from a particular manufacturer's cable sets but grey card or other paving by others suppliers could be used.

A walled goods yard

Back in steam days when goods yards were to be found all over the rail network, quite a lot of them that were located in large town or city centres were surrounded by high walls or warehouses or a combination of both.

On a small goods yard layout I built recently, I decided to give it an urban setting rather than the more common rural setting seen on many small layouts. So how would I make the high walls that give the yard its character? The answer came from the Skaledale range which has a set of retaining walls, both straight and sloped, realistically moulded and finished in typical red brick style. Of course, these wall sections are actually intended to line railway cuttings, as the catalogue and pack illustrations show. However, sometimes models can be switched to other uses – in this case as a free-standing wall.

I used straight-topped wall section R8730 and two were needed for my goods yard. The rest of the background was to be taken up by warehouses. For a longer layout you could use more than two sections as desired.

Follow the photographs to see how the setting was developed.

■ Figure 1 The backscene for the layout is a length of hardboard, in this case 6 inches (15cm) high. The hardboard is painted sky blue first – with some emulsion paint – and some suitable background buildings are cut from background sheets available from model shops. The office block on the left is cut from an old model kit catalogue, which is another source for backscene items. As you can see, two treetops are also cut out and glued in place. As the wall will take up a lot of the height, you only need the upper parts of buildings on the backscene. Here the first section of Skaledale retaining wall is being glued to the backboard.

■ Figure 2 The wall sections are now glued in place and the first warehouse, made from plastic kit parts, is also in place on the left. Note the gap left between the wall and the warehouse, to allow road vehicles to enter the goods yard. Note also the poster stuck on the wall.

■ Figure 3 You can conceal the join between the two wall sections by having ivy growing up and over the top of the wall. This is done using the R8839 Skale Scenics fibre clusters, stretched in strips and glued up the wall. The last piece is glued to the parapet of the wall.

■ Figure 4 More foliage and some teased out R8863 field grass are used for growth at the foot of the wall. Ordinary card, painted grey, is used to depict the road surface by the track. R8808 ScaleScenics gravel is used to cover the joins in the card.

■ Figure 5 The finished setting with a GWR 'Terrier' arriving in the yard. Note crew added to the loco cab and a guard figure in the brake van.

Figure 1

Figure 2

Figure 3

Figure 4

Figure 5

Appendix

Appendix

Magazines

- *British Railway Modelling*. Warner Publishing Group.
- *Continental Modeller*. Peco Publications & Publicity, website: (www.peco-uk.com). This magazine covers overseas modelling only.
- *ModelRail*. Emap Active, website: **www.modelrail.com**
- *Model Railway Journal*. Wild Swan Publications. This magazine covers the more advanced 'fine scale' scene.
- *Model Trains International*. Kristall Productions, website: **www.model-trainsinternational.co.uk**. This magazine covers both British and overseas modelling.
- *Railway Modeller*. Peco Publications & Publicity, website: **www.peco-uk.com**
- *Hornby Magazine*. Ian Allan Publishing, website: **www.hornbymagazine.com**

In addition to the above, the railway news magazine *Rail Express* includes a model section in each issue.

Hornby Collectors' Club

This club is open to all collectors and operators of Hornby model railways. It publishes the bi-monthly *Collector*, covering all Hornby model rail subjects. The UK subscription (in 2010) is £24.50 a year, payable to Hornby Hobbies. Applications to Hornby Collectors' Club, PO Box 25, Melton Mowbray, Leicestershire LE13 IZG.

Hornby Catalogue

This comes out in January of each year and is priced at £8.50 (2010 edition). 192 pages, full colour. It details all of Hornby's products. It can be bought either online at www.hornby.com or from most model shops.

CD ROM

- 88125 *Hornby step-by-step guide to Railway Modelling*. Packed with hints and advice on laying out buildings, scenics, operating, etc. and shown opposite.

Specialist suppliers

All the Hornby products mentioned in this book are generally available from model railway shops in Britain. It is useful, however, to get the latest catalogue and any brochures published by Hornby to check out new products. Plastic building kits by German manufacturers, and scenic materials from Noch, Busch, and Woodland Scenics are also available at larger model shops. For other products mentioned in the book the following addresses can be contacted:

Brush-it-On, 246 Albion Street
Wall Heath, Kingswinford
West Midlands DY6 0JR, UK

Merkur, Sipp and other German scenic products
International Models, Plas Cadfor
Llywyngwril, Gwynedd LL37 2LA, UK
www.internationalmodels.net

Foreign magazines
If you model overseas railways, the following magazines are available from some specialist model shops and include articles useful for scenic modelling, applicable to the respective countries.

USA
Model Railroader, Railroad Model Craftsman

Germany
Eisenbahn Kurier, Eisenbahn Journal

France
Loco-Revue

step-by-step GUIDE
RAILWAY MODELLING

NEW   R 8125

The Hornby Step-By-Step Guide to

Railway Modelling...

Hornby's new 'Step-by-step Guide to Railway Modelling' CD-Rom is the perfect resource to establish, evolve and complement your hobby skills - whether you are starting out, an enthusiast or an experienced modeller.

Railway modelling is a creative hobby that can provide 'satisfaction for a lifetime' but it can be particularly difficult and frustrating when 'getting started'. This CD-Rom is designed to help guide the beginner or novice in the hobby to move beyond the train set and take his or her first practical steps to building a layout.

You do not have to be a highly skilled modeller in order to produce good layouts. It can be all too easy to become disillusioned by advanced modellers who may suggest you have to 'scratch build' all of your stock and track in order to be recognised as a 'true modeller'. Hornby's complete off-the-shelf 'ready-to-run' scale railway system is a good cost effective alternative to buying and building the equivalent models in kits and enables beginners in particular to get started in much less time.

This innovative CD-Rom, produced by modelling experts, adopts a simple step-by-step approach, providing advice, explaining methods and demonstrating techniques by walking you logically through key tasks and activities. The interactive CD-Rom is designed to help inspire and guide you towards your perfect model railway.

The CD-Rom includes:

Where do I start?

Careful planning is essential. This chapter introduces types of train set and circuit layout types, sizes, locations and budgets. Also included is a historical timeline highlighting how some modellers go about selecting a period of time upon which to base their models.

Baseboards and track

Getting the foundations right. This chapter explains types of baseboard, materials required and provides detailed step-by-step guides on 'Building Solid Top Frame Baseboards' and 'Laying the track'.

Buildings and scenics

Setting the scene. This chapter explains aspects of scenic and structural modelling starting with planning and observation. It goes on to provide detailed step-by-step guides on 'Construction', 'Shaping the land' and 'Scenic finish'. A guide to 'Buildings and structures' coupled with sections on building kits and 'adding life' helps complete the chapter.

Wiring the layout

Powering up. This chapter introduces wiring and starts with the importance of electrical safety. It continues with a simple explanation of electricity, types of circuit, signal and point operation and concludes with advice on using more than one controller and digital command control (DCC).

Taking stock

Getting your stock rolling. This chapter introduces ready-to-run models and locomotive kits and follows with advice on detailing including couplings, weathering and adding even more detail to your models.

System Requirements

The CD-Rom is designed to run on industry standard IBM PC and Apple MAC compatible computers. These are guidelines for the successful running of the software.

Minimum: PC Pentium II 300MHz, 64Mb RAM to 128Mb RAM, 20Mb Free Disk Space, 16Mb Graphics Card, 8 x CD-Rom, SoundBlaster 128 Compatible Card, Windows 98, 2000, Me, XP

Recommended: PC Pentium III 800MHz, 64Mb RAM to 128Mb RAM, 20Mb Free Disk Space, 32Mb Graphics Card, 16 x CD-Rom, SoundBlaster 128 Compatible Card, Windows 98, 2000, Me, XP

Hornby would like to thank the Editor and Staff of British Railway Modelling for their assistance in the compiling of this CD-Rom

150

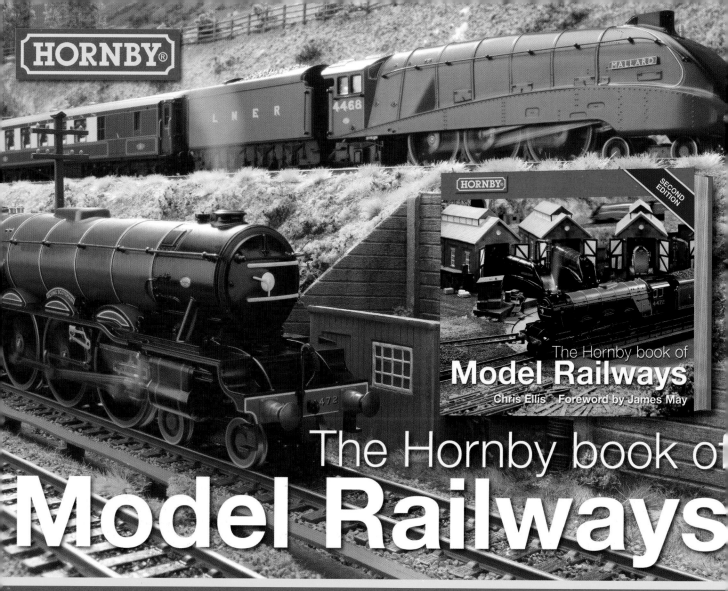

HORNBY®

MALLARD

4468

The Hornby book of
Model Railways

The Hornby book of
Model Railways

The Hornby Book of Model Railways is packed with hints and tips for easy layout building, scenic and structure modelling, track laying and wiring, extra detailing, and all other aspects of the model railway hobby. The book also outlines the Hornby range and explains digital command control systems in full. Covering the basics for beginners, with additional projects for more advanced modellers, it will appeal to Hornby enthusiasts and indeed anyone beginning in the model railway hobby. This includes all young modellers (and their parents!) who start with a Hornby train set.

CONWAY

9781844860951 | £14.99 | 176pp | 190x210mm

Model railway shops

ENGLAND

Avon Antics 8 Fairfax Street, Bristol, BS1 3DB Tel: 01179 273744 **Bath Model Centre** 2 Lower Borough Walls, Bath, BA1 1QR Tel: 01225 460115 **Modelmania of Bristol** 13 Clouds Hill Road, St George, Bristol, BS5 7LD Tel: 01179 559819 **Richard's Railways** 120 High Street, Yatton, Bristol, BS49 4DH Tel: 01934 876328 **Trains Of Bristol** 20 West Street, Bedminster, BS3 3LG Tel: 01179 872052

Bedfordshire Dunstable Model Centre 25 West Street, Dunstable, LU6 1SL Tel: 01582 662566 **MR & ME** Unit 7, Saxon Centre, Bedford Road, Kempston, MK42 8PP Tel: 01234 852780 **MRE Model Shop** 26 High Street, Leighton Buzzard, LU7 1EA Tel: 01525 377588 **N Gauge Lines** 101 Harrowden Road, Bedford, MK42 0RT Tel: 01234 261482 **Thameshead Models** 101 Harrowden Road, Bedford, MK42 0RT Tel: 01234 261482

Berkshire Brunswick Railways Ltd. 5 The Cuttings, 120 High Street, Hungerford, RG17 0LU Tel: 01488 686622 **Child Beale Trading Co. Ltd** Walliscote House, High Street, Whitchurch on Thames, RG8 9NH Tel: 01491 671388 **Marlow Donkey Railways / MDR Direct** The Old Bank, High Street, Cookham, Maidenhead, SL6 9SJ Tel: 01628 819262 **Modelzone** Broad Street Mall, Reading, RG1 7QH Tel: 0118 9586109 **Timemachine** 32 Westborough Road, Maidenhead, SL6 4AR Tel: 01628 622603 **WJ Daniel & Co Ltd** 120 Peascod Street, Windsor, SL4 1DP Tel: 01753 862106

Buckinghamshire Cramarrs 18 Octagon Parade, High Wycombe, HP11 2HU Tel: 01494 523550 **Garden Railway Specialists** Station Studio, 6 Summerleys Road, Princes Risborough, HP27 9DT Tel: 01844 345158 **Hunts of Marlow** 14 Spittal Street, Marlow SL7 1DB Tel: 01628 488228 **Model Junction** 21 The Parade, Bourne End, Buckinghamshire, SL8 5SB Tel: 01628 528617 **Model Motors** 21 The Parade, Bourne End, SL8 5SB Tel: 01628 528617 **Model World** 3 London Road, Newport Pagnall, MK16 0HA Tel: 01908 612983 **Modelzone** 17 Acorn Walk, The Centre, Milton Keynes, MK9 3AD Tel: 01908 605692 **Transport Treasures** 2 London Road, Aston Clinton, Aylesbury, HP22 5HQ Tel: 01296 631002 **Wycombe Models & Engineering** 1 Gomm Road, High Wycombe, HP13 7DJ Tel: 01494 447941 **Modelzone** 17 Acorn Walk, The Centre, Milton Keynes, MK9 3AD Tel: 01908 605692

Cambridgeshire Berbarda Hobbies 91 Norfolk Street, Wisbech, PE13 2LF Tel: 01945 467740 **Broadway Junction** The Coach House, 9 The Broadway, St. Ives, Huntingdon, PE17 4BX Tel: 01480 464684 **City Cycle Centre** 7 Market Street, Ely, CB7 4PB Tel: 01353 663131 **Glendale Junction** 5 New Row, Deeping St James, Peterborough, PE6 8NA Tel: 01778 343183 **Nene Valley Railway Ent Ltd** Wansford Station, Sibbington, Peterborough, PE8 6LR Tel: 01780 784444 **Peggies Pandora** 10 Cross Keys, Market Square St.Neots, PE19 2AU Tel: 01480 403580 **R&D Models** 23 Burleigh Street, Cambridge, CB1 1DG Tel: 01223 360249 **Sports & Fashions Ltd** 51 High Street, Huntingdon, PED18 6AQ Tel: 01480 454541 **Trains4U** Unit 20, St Davids Square, Fengate, Peterborough, PE1 5QA Tel: 01733 895989

Cheshire Arts & Crafts Studio 16 St Michaels Row, The Grosvenor Shopping Centre, Chester, CH1 1EF Tel: 01244 324900 **Cheshire Models** 37 Sunderland Street, Macclesfield, SK11 6JL Tel: 01625 511646 **Deans Toys & Cycles** Lawton Street, Congleton, CW12 1RT Tel: 01260 273277 **ER Dean** Lawton Street, Congleton, CW12 1RT Tel: 01260 273277 **Haslington Models** 134 Crewe Road, Haslington, Crewe, CW1 5RQ Tel: 01270 589079 **Modelzone** 71-73 Bridge Street Row East Chester, CH1 1NW Tel: 01244 324900 **Railway Junction** 187 Orford Lane, Warrington, WA2 7BA Tel: 01925 632209 **Trident Trains** 10 The Craft Arcade, Dagfields, Craft and Antique Centre, Crewe Road, Nantwich, CW5 7LG, Tel: 01270 842400 **Trident Trains at Dagfields** Crafts & Antique Centre, Dagfields Farm, Walgherton, Nr Nantwich, CW5 7LG, Tel: 01270 842 400 **Waltons of Altrincham** 30 Stamford Street, Altrincham, WA14 1EY Tel: 0161 928 5940 **Wigan & Warrington Model Centres** 33 Horsemarket Street, Warrington, WA1 1TS Tel: 01925 574539 **Modelzone** 71-73 Bridge Street Row East, Chester, CH1 1NW Tel: 01244 324900

Cleveland Redcar Models & Hobbies 130 High Street, Redcar, TS19 3DH Tel: 01642 494912 **Stockton Modeller Ltd** 10 Silver Street, Stockton-on-Tees, TS18 1SX Tel: 07967 440108 **Walker's Model Railways** 37 Charles Street, Redcar, TS10 3HP Tel: 01642 481884

Devon Bodmin & Wenford Railway Bodmin General Station, Lostwithiel Road, Bodmin, PL31 1AQ Tel: 01208 73666 **Eddy's Of Helston Ltd** 21 Meneage Street, Helston, TR13 8AA Tel: 01326 572787 **Great Western Scale Models** 5 Pentowan Road, Loggans, Hayle, TR27 5AR Tel: 01736 757679 **Hidden Valley Adventure Park** Tredidon, St Thomas, Launceston, PL15 8SJ **Hobbyclub**

Ltd 101 Trelowarren Street, Camborne, TR15 2AZ Tel: 01209 212758 **Hudsons Scale Models** 65 Causewayhead, Penzance, TR18 2SR Tel: 01736 362062 **Inter-City Models** 9 Celtic House, Harbour Road, Porthleven, TR13 9JY Tel: 01326 569200 **Kernow Model Rail Centre** 98 Trelowarren Street, Camborne, TR14 8AN Tel: 01209 714099 **Mevagissey Model Railway** Meadow Street, Mevagissey, PL26 6UL Tel: 01726 842457 **Model Master** 2-4 Calenick Street, Truro, TR1 2SF Tel: 01872 241564

Cumbria Alston Model Railway Centre Unit 1, Station Yard Workshops, Alston, CA9 3HN Tel: 01434 382100/382169 **Bowness Models,** 26 Lake Road Bowness, Windermere, LA23 3AP Tel: 015394 44090 **C&tM Models** 1 Crosby Street, Carlisle, CA1 1DQ Tel: 01228 514689 **Crafty Hobbies** Unit 49-50 Barrow, Indoor Market, Duke Street, Barrow in Furness, LA14 1HU Tel: 01229 820759 **Hunter's Toys and Models** 4 Kinmont Arcade, Off Fisher Street, Carlisle, CA3 8RF Tel: 01228 527700 **O'Loughlins Toys and Models** 44 Finkle Street, Kendal, LA9 4AB Tel: 01539 723264 **Photo & Hobby Center** 255 Rawlinson Street, Barrow in Furness, LA14 1DH Tel: 01229 822905

Derbyshire AB Gee of Ripley Ltd Asher House, Asher Lane Business Park, Ripley, DE5 3SW Tel: 01773 570444 **Bakewell Model Centre** 1 Portland Square, Bakewell, S45 1HA Tel: 01629 815677 **C&B Models** 103 Normanton Road, Derby, DE1 2GG Tel: 01332 367 506 **Frearsons Ltd** 10 Bridge Street, Belper, DE56 1AX Tel: 01773 823244 **High Peak Heating Supplies** Towngate, Bradwell, High Peak, S33 9JXTel: 01433 620577 **KMB Models** 56a Alexandra Road, Swadlincote, DE11 9AY Tel: 01283 215138 **Malc's Models** 170A Nottingham Road, Ilkeston, DE7 5AB Tel: 07786 896807 **Midland Railway Trust Ltd** Butterley Station, Ripley, DE5 3LW Tel: 01905 776681 **Modelzone** Level 1 South Mall, Westfield Shopping Centre, Derby, DE1 2PG Tel: 01332 209637 **Trainlines of Derby Ltd** 107 Nottingham Road, Derby, DE1 3QR Tel: 01332 343943 **WD Models** 15 Chatsworth Road, Chesterfield, S40 2AH Tel: 01246 208244

Devon Antics 30 Royal Parade, Plymouth, PL1 1DU Tel: 01752 221851 **Austins of Newton Abbot** Wolborough Street, Newton Abbot, TQ12 2DU Tel: 01626 201117 **Bekra R/C** 91 Queen Street, Newton Abbot, TQ12 2BG Tel: 01626 334884 **Browsers** 1&2 The Strand, Exmouth, EX8 1HL Tel: 01395 265010 **Buffers Model Railways** Axminster-Chard Road, Colston Cross, Axminster, Devon EX13 7NF Tel: 01297 35557 **Dartmoor Railway Model Supplies** Okehampton Station, Okehampton EX20 1EJ

Tel: 01837 55330 **Devon Railway Centre** The Old Station, Bickleigh, Tiverton, Devon, EX16 8RG Tel: 01884 855671 **Exeter Model Centre** 39 Sidwell Street, Exeter, EX4 6NS Tel: 01392 435118 **Gliddon Toys** 4 Church Street, Sidmouth, EX10 8LZ Tel: 01395 516695 **Modelzone** 22 Frankfort Gate, City Centre, Plymouth, PL1 1QD Tel: 01752 263133 **Model Megastore** Platform 1 Models, 36 Winner Street, Paignton, TQ3 3BQ Tel: 01803 555003 **North Devon Models** 72 Boutport Street, Barnstaple, EX31 1SR Tel: 01271 377386 **Peco Model Shop** Underleys, Beer Seaton, EX12 3NA Tel: 01297 20580 **Railway Expressway Models** The Station, Buckfastleigh, TQ11 0DZ Tel: 01364 643113 **Tavyside Model Supplies** 11A Mount Tavy Road, Tavistock, PL19 9JB Tel: 01822 612741 **Teign Models** 3 Higher Brimley, Teignmouth, TQ14 8JS Tel: 01626 772466 **The Lookout** 75 High Street, Totnes, TQ9 5PB Tel: 01803 840111 **The Model Shop** 4 St David's Hill, Exeter, EX4 3RG Tel: 01392 421906 **Trago Mills Regional Shopping Centre** Stover, Newton Abbot, TQ12 6JD Tel: 01626 821111 **Vintage Toy & Train Shop** Sidmouth Antiques Centre, All Saints Road, Sidmouth, EX10 8ES Tel: 01395 512588

Dorset **Bournemouth Model Railway Centre** 329-331 Holdenhurst Road, Bournemouth, BH8 8BT Tel: 01202 309872 **Frank Herring & Sons** 27 High West Street, Dorchester, DT1 1UP Tel: 01305 264449 **Howleys** 5 Frederick Place, Weymouth, DT4 8HQ Tel: 01305 779255 **Premier Gauge Railways** Brick House, Kington Magna, Gillingham, SP8 5EG Tel: 01747 838359 **Setchfields Models** 21-25 High Street,Poole, BH15 1AB Tel: 01202 673300 **W Frost & Co Ltd** 44 South Street, Bridport, Dorset, DT6 3NN Tel: 01308 422271

Durham **C&G Model Railways** 95 Parkgate, Darlington, DL1 1RZ Tel: 01325 381085 **Durham Railway Models** Indoor Market Place, Durham Tel: 07930 129553 **Model Active** The Old Chapel, Chester Moor, Chester-le-Street, DH2 3RJ Tel: 0191 387 4338 **Stevenson's** 53 Hope Street, Crook, DL15 9HU Tel: 01388 767 937

East Sussex **Bluebell Railway plc** Sheffield Park Station, Sheffield Park, Uckfield, TN22 3QL Tel: 01825 723777 **J Morris Models** 80 Manor Road, North Lancing, BN15 0HD Tel: 01903 754850 **Loco Notion Models** 131 Coast Road, Peacehaven, BN10 8UR Tel: 07710 215566 **Modelzone** 37 West Street, Brighton, BN21 2RE Tel: 01273 326790 **Modelzone** 68 Seaside Road, Eastbourne, BN21 3PD Tel: 01323 411736 **Silverhill Models & Toys** 383 London Road, St Leonards on Sea, TN37 6PA Tel: 01424 431133 **The Hobby Box** 8 Framfield Road, Uckfield,

ETN22 5AG Tel: 01825 765296 **Train Times** 37 Seaside, Eastbourne, BN22 7NB Tel: 01323 722026 **Valelink Ltd** 26 Queens Road, Brighton, BN1 3XA Tel: 01273 202906

East Yorkshire **53A Models** 430 Hessle Road, Hull, HU3 3SE Tel: 01482 227777 **Baxters** 20-22 Hepworths Arcade, Silver Street, Hull, East Yorkshire, HU1 1JU Tel: 01482 229779 **Croppers Models** 17 Lansdowne Road, Bridlington, YO15 2QU Tel: 01262 677231 **The Model Shop** 179 Ferensway, Hull, HU1 3UA Tel: 01482 329199 **Modelzone** Unit 21, Stephens Shopping Centre, Hull HU2 8LN Tel: 01482 224640

Essex **Braintree Model Railways** 106 South Street Braintree, CM7 3QQ Tel: 01376 348004 **Clacton Models** 30A St. Osyth Road,Clacton on Sea, CO15 3BW Tel: 01255 688433 **Colchester Model Centre** 1 Albion Grove, Winchester Road, Colchester, CO2 7RZ Tel: 01206 795627 **DJ's Models** 1176 London Road,Leigh on Sea, S9 2AH Tel: 01702 471196 **Hedingham Models** 7 Market Street, Phoenix Shopping Centre, Braintree, CM7 3YA Tel: 01376 320522 **Heki (Blackwells of Hawkwell)** The Old Maltings, 5 Weir Pond Road, Rochford, SS4 1AH Tel: 01702 542627 or 541555 **Hobby House** 34 Hullbridge Road, South Woodham Ferrers, Chelmsford, CM3 5PL Tel: 01245 320607 **John Dutfield for Model Railways** Wards Yard, 133 Springfield Park Road, Chelmsford, CM2 6EE Tel: 01245 494455 **Modelzone** Unit 96, Lakeside Shopping Centre, Thurrock, RM20 2ZG Tel: 01708 869412 **Plus Daughters** Unit 4, Trafalgar House, Thames Industrial Estate, Princess Margaret Road, East Tilbury, RM18 8RH Tel: 01375 488003 **Rickatrack Model Railways** 347 Victoria Avenue, Southend-on-Sea, SS2 6NH Tel: 01702 346079 **Roneo Models** 32 Roneo Corner, Hornchurch, RM12 4TN Tel: 01708 442836

Gloucestershire **Antics** 79 Northgate Street, Gloucester, GL1 2AG Tel: 01452 410693 **Antics** 49 High Street, Stroud, GL5 1AN Tel: 01453 765920 **Bourton Model Railways** Box Bush, High Street, Bourton on the Water, GL54 2AN Tel: 01451 820686 **Cheltenham Model Centre** 39 High Street, Cheltenham, Gloucestershire, GL50 1DY Tel: 01242 234644 **Dean Sidings** 41 High Street, Lydney, Forest of Dean, GL15 5DD Tel: 01594 842318 **Garden Railway Centres Ltd** Capel Orchard, London Road, Cheltenham, GL52 6UZ Tel: 01242 519770 **Gloucester Model Warehouse** 49 Carlton Road, Gloucester, GL1 5DZ Tel: 01452 526490

Greater Manchester **All Gauges Model Railways** Unit 15, Reliance Trading Est, Reliance Street, Newton Heath, M40 3AG Tel: 0161 682 0580 **Arcadia** 67 Rochdale

Road, Shaw, Oldham, OL2 7JT Tel: 01706 882900 **Bolton Model Mart** 58 Great Moor Street, Bolton, BL1 1SN Tel: 01204 382282 **Bury Steam Loco Co** 87 Glebelands Road, Prestwich, Greater Manchester, M25 1WF Tel:0161 761 6630 **Cheshire Model Supplies Ltd** 96 Shawheath, Stockport, SK3 8BP Tel: 0161 480 2804 **East Lancashire Railway** Bolton Street Station, Bury, BL9 0EY Tel: 0161 763 4408 **F&S Scale Models** 227 Droylsden Road, Audenshaw, M34 5RT Tel: 0161 370 3235 **G&I Model Railways** 58 Market St, Wigan, WN1 1HX Tel: 01942 494724 **Ian Allan Bookshop** 5 Gateway House, Piccadilly Approach, M1 2GH Tel: 0161 237 9840 **Modelzone** 209 Deansgate, M3 3NM Tel: 0161 834 3972 **Norman Wisenden**, 95 Chew Valley Road, Greenfield, Oldham, OL3 7JJ Tel: 01457 876045 **Pilkington Cycles** 101 The Rock, Bury, BL9 0NB Tel: 0161 764 2723 **SRA Models** 1 Mersey Square, Stockport, SK1 1NU Tel: 0161 429 9083 **The Model Shop** 695 Ripponden Road, Oldham, OL1 4SA Tel: 0161 624 8415 **The Toy Shop** 138a Wright Road, Horwich, Bolton, BL6 7HU Tel: 01204 669782 **Toolbox Toys & Models** 81 Stockport Road, Denton, M34 6DD Tel: 0161 336 2460 **Wigan & Warrington Model Centres** 58 Market Street, Wigan, WN1 1HX Tel: 01942 494724 or 245683

Hampshire **Alton Model Centre** 7A Normandy Street, Alton, GU34 1DD Tel: 01420 542244 **Concorde Models** 179 Victoria Road, Aldershot, GU11 1JU Tel: 01252 326825 **Footplate Railway Models** 7 St James Road, Shirley, Southampton, SO15 5FB Tel: 02380 771546 **Fratton Model Centre (St.Petrocks Models UK)**171-173 Fratton Road, Fratton, Portsmouth, PO1 5ET Tel: 02392 827117 **Mainly Planes 'N' Trains** 6 Ashdown Road, Hiltingbury, Chandlersford, SO53 5RD Tel: 023 8025 3058 **Milford Models & Hobbies** 48 High Sreet, Milford On Sea, Lymington, SO41 0QD Tel: 01590 642112 **Model Collectors Corner**, 117 New Road Portsmouth, PO2 7QS Tel: 02392 653100 **Modelzone** Unit 56, Festival Place, Basingstoke, RG21 7BF Tel: 01256 844787 **Modelzone** 85 Above Bar Street, Southampton, SO14 7FG Tel: 02380 338265 **Moors Valley Railway** Moors Valley Country Park, Horton Road, Ashley Heath, Ringwood, BH24 2ET Tel: 01425 471415 **Park Trains and Models** 50 Northam Road, Southampton, SO15 0HW Tel: 02380 369997 **Patronics** Unit 21, Solent Business Centre, Miullbrook Road, West, Southampton, SO15 0HW Tel: 02380 369997 **Southampton Model Centre** 13 Junction Road, Totton, Southampton, SO40 9HG Tel: 02380 667317 **Tony's Trains & Models** 2a Torrington Road, Hillsea, Portsmouth, PO2 0TP Tel: 01705 653545 **Waterlooviller Model Centre**

34 Wellington Way, Waterlooville, PO7 7ED Tel: 02392 259186 **Wicor Models** 20 West Street, Portchester, PO16 9UZ Tel: 023 9235 1160 **Woodgreen Model Railways** Silver Birches, Hale Road, Woodgreen, Fordingbridge SP6 2AJ Tel: 01725 511977

Herefordshire Hereford Model Centre 4 Commercial Road, Hereford, HR1 2BA Tel: 01432 352809 **Kenwater Rail-Ways** Kenwater House, Bridge Street, Leominster, HR6 8DX Tel: 01568 614336 **Martins Models & Crafts** 26 West Street, Leominster, HR6 8ES Tel: 01568 613782 **Martins Models Garden Railways**, The Forge Hatton Gardens, Kington HR5 3RB Tel: **Totally Trains** 1 Cantilupe Court, Cantilupe Road, Ross on Wye, HR9 7AN Tel: 01989 567577 **Toybox** Homend Mews, The Homend, Ledbury, HR8 1BN, Tel: 01531 632189

Hertfordshire Albanrail Big G-scale 18 Ben Austins, Redbourn, St Albans, AL3 7DP Tel: 01582 792013 **BH Enterprises** 68 Meadow Road, Garston, WD2 6JA Tel: 01923 672809 **Junction 20 Models** 51 High Street, Kings Langley, WD4 9HU Tel: 01923 270247 **K.S's World of Models** 19 Middle Row, Stevenage, Hertfordshire, SG1 3AW Tel: 08707 572286 **Model Images** 56 Station Road, Letchworth, SG6 3BE Tel: 01462 684859 **The Toy Shop** 25 High Street, Royston, SG8 9AA Tel: 01763 243270 **Time Tunnel Models** 3 Market Place, New Town Centre, Stevenage, SG1 1DH Tel: 01438 742665

Kent Ballards 54 Grosvenor Road, Tunbridge Wells, TN1 2AS Tel: 01892 531803 **Chalk Garden Rail** 4 Brewhouse Yard, Gravesend, DA12 2EJ Tel: 01474 351672 **East Kent Models** 89 High Street, Whitstable, CT5 1AY Tel: 01227 770777 **EM Models** 51 Camden Road, Tunbridge Wells, TN1 2QD Tel: 01892 536689 **Hythe (Kent) Models** 153a High Street, Hythe, CT21 5JL Tel: 01303 267236 **Kent Garden Railways** 68 High Street, St Mary Cray, Orpington BR5 3NH Tel: 01689 891668 **Manklows** 44 Seal Road, Sevenoaks, TN14 5AR Tel: 01732 454952 **Model World** The Court Yard, Newnham Court Centre, Bearsted Road, Maidstone, ME14 5LH Tel: 01622 735855 **Modelzone** 73 Lower Thames Walk, Bluewater, Greenhithe, DA9 9SL, Tel: 01322 623890 **Modelzone** 6 Stewards Walk, Liberty Shopping Centre, Romford, RM1 3RL Tel: 01708 732875 **Modelzone** Unit 202, Chequers Centre, Maidstone, ME15 6AR Tel: 01622 691184 **Ramsgate Models** 74 Queens Street, Ramsgate, CT11 9ER Tel: **Rons Model Rail & Diecast** 53 High Street, Rochester, Kent, ME1 1LN Tel: 01634 827992 **The Hobby Shop** 122 West Street, Faversham, ME13 7JB Tel: 01795 531666 **The Signal Box** 382-386 High Street, Rochester, ME1 1DQ Tel: 01634

826370 **Turner's Models** 14 London Road, Dover, CT17 0ST Tel: 01304 203711 **Whites Stone Street, Cranbrook, TN17 3HE Tel: 01580 713298

Lancashire Bay Models Unit 5, Carnforth Station, Carnforth, LA5 9TR Tel: 01524 730101 **Chris Brierley Models** 53 York Street, Heywood, OL10 4NR Tel: 01706 365812 **JH Models** Parkhill Barn, Garstang, Preston, PR3 1HB Tel: 01995 601289 **Lancaster City Models** 11 Chapel Street, Lancaster, LA1 1PD Tel: 01524 63043 **Mercer & Sons Ltd** 21-27 Northgate, Blackburn, BB2 1JT Tel: 01254 587000 **Model Rail** 122-124, Hebrew Road, Duke Bar, Burnley, BB10 1LR Tel: 01282 451958 **Pendle / Porter Wynn Models** 7 Woone Lane, Clitheroe, BB7 2QF Tel: 01200 442409 **Red Bank Models** 201 Central Drive, Blackpool, FY1 5ED Tel: 01253 751537 **Station Models** Unit 2, The Gateway Building, Carnforth Station, Warton Road, Carnforth, LA5 9TR Tel: 01524 847955 **Stewarts Model Centre** 174 Union Road, Oswaldtwistle, Accrington, BB5 3EG Tel: 01254 384433 **The Model Shop** 169 Old Street, Ashton under Lyne, OL6 7SQ Tel: 0161 330 6047 **The Train Shop** 23 Pedder Street, Morecambe, LA4 5DY Tel: 01524 413112 **Tower Models** 44 Cookson Street, Blackpool, FY1 3ED Tel: 01253 623797 **Toys 2 Save Collectables** Marsh Mill, Craft Village, Thornton Cleveleys, Blackpool, FY5 4JZ Tel: 01253 855905 **Transport Models** Unit 1, Oyston Mill, Strand Road, Preston, PR1 8UR Tel: 01772 733644

Leicestershire ACME Model Products 48 Highgate Road, Sileby, LE12 7PP Tel: 01509 812177 **Arbon & Watts Ltd** 39 Sherrard Street, Melton Mowbray, LE13 1XH Tel: 01664 850010 **Central Models & Hobbies** 2 Winchester Avenue, Off Blaby By-pass, Blaby, LE8 4GZ Tel: 0116 277 3013 **Great Central Railway plc** Great Central Road, Loughborough, LE11 1RW Tel: 01509 230726 **Hobbybahn** Dadlington, CV13 6JD Tel: 01455 213099 **Keith's Model Railways** 2 Holyrood Drive, Countesthorpe, LE8 3TR Tel: 0116 2778634 **Syston Trains** 1246 Melton Road, Syston, Leicester, LE7 2HB Tel: 0116 269 8848 **The Hobby Horse** 32 The Banks, Barrow upon Soar, LE12 8NL Tel: 01509 620318 **The Signal Box** 1 Albion Street, Anstey, Leicester, LE7 7DD Tel: 0116 236 2901

Lincolnshire Access Models 16 Market Place, Grantham, NG31 6LJ Tel: 01636 673116 **Arbon & Watts Ltd** 96 Westgate, Grantham, NG31 6LE Tel: 01476 400014 **Ashtree Enterprises** Ashtree House, 33 Nettleton Road, Caistor, LN7 6NJ Tel: 01472 851736 **B&H Models** 13 Corporation Street, Lincoln, LN2 1HL Tel: 01522 538717 **Blossom Hall Trains** The Old Forge, Sots Hole Bank,

Holbeach St Matthew, Spalding, PE5 8JE Tel: 01406 701612 **Caistor Loco** 8 Market Place, Caistor, LN7 6TW Tel: 07773 145329 **Digitrans Ltd** The Stables, Digby Manor, North Street, Digby, Lincoln, LN4 3LY Tel: 01526 328633 **Dines of Scartho** 21 Waltham Road, Scartho, Grimsby, DN33 2LY Tel: 01472 877462 **Fraction Models** 10 Roman Bank, Skegness, PE25 2RU Tel: 01754 760077 **Granary Models** 31 High Street, Swineshead, Nr Boston, PE20 3LH Tel: 01205 820115 **Hobbins Models** 408-410A High Street, Lincoln, LN5 7TE Tel: 01522 531084 **J&N Models MU5** New Market Hall, Louth, LN11 9PY Tel: 01507 600501 **Masons Models** 20 New Road, Spalding, PE11 1DQ, Tel: 01775 722456 **Models & Hobbies** 7b East St Mary's Gate, Grimsby, DN31 1LH Tel: 01472 347088 **Shermans Model Shop** 19 Dunstall Street, Scunthorpe, DN15 6LD Tel: 01724 842439 **Spalding Models & Collectables** 17 The Cresent, Spalding, PE11 1AF Tel: 01775 713270

London Braley Hobby Supplies 141 Little Ealing Lane, Ealing, W5 4EJ Tel: 020 8567 3371 **EF Russ** 101 Battersea Rise, SW11 1HW Tel: 020 7228 6319 **Engine 'N' Tender** 19 Spring Lane, Woodside, SE25 4SP Tel: 020 8654 0386 **Harrods Limited** 87-135 Brompton Road, Knightsbridge, SW1X 7XL Tel: 020 7225 6781 **Hobby Stop** 95 Station Road, Chingford, E4 7BU Tel: 020 8529 7377 **Home of 'O' Gauge** 528 Kingston Road, Raynes Park, SW20 8DT Tel: 020 8540 8808 **Ian Allan Bookshop** 45-46 Lower Marsh, Waterloo, SE1 7RG Tel: 020 740 12100 **Janes Trains** 35 London Road, Tooting, SW17 9JR Tel: 020 8640 1569 **Jennings Models** 244-248 Hertford Road, Hillingdon, Enfield, EN3 5BL Tel: 020 8804 1767 **Just Trains** 2A Chatterton Road, Bromley, BR2 9QN Tel: 020 8249 3949 **Modelzone** Unit 1, 24 St Nicholas Centre, St Nicholas Way, Sutton, SM1 1AW Tel: 020 8643 5300 **Modelzone** 272 The Glades, High Street, Bromley, Greater London BR1 1DN Tel: 020 8313 1735 **Modelzone** Unit 31, Centrale Shopping Centre, Croydon, Greater London Tel: 020 8688 6519 **Modelzone** 202 High Holborn, WC1V 6JS Tel: 020 7405 6285 **North London Models** 474 Hornsey Road, N19 4EF Tel: 020 7281 7877 **Norwood Junction Models** 3 Orton Buildings, Portland Road, SE25 4UD Tel: 020 8653 4943 **Richardsons of Feltham** 6-7 Rochester Parade, High Street, Feltham, TW13 4DX Tel: 020 8890 4399/9946 **The Engine Shed** 745 High Road, Leytonstone, E11 4QS Tel: 020 8539 3950 **Wheels of Steel** Grays Antique Market, 1-7 Davies Mews, W1Y 1AR Tel: 020 7629 2813 or 020 8505 0750 **Wilton Cycle & Wireless Co** 28 Upper Tachbrook Street, SW1V 1SW Tel: 020 883 41367

Merseyside DKG Hobbies 14 Princes Street, Southport PR8 1EZ Tel: 01704 500630 Fireside Miniatures 206 Liscard Road, Liscard, Wallasey, CH44 5TN Tel: 0151 6911683 Formby Models, 77-79 Gores Lane, Formby, L37 7DE Tel: 01704 870432 Hatton's 364-368 Smithdown Road, Liverpool, L15 5AN Tel: 0151 733 3655 Kit Stop 20 Oxton Road, Birkenhead, L41 2OJ Tel: 0151 647 9067 Model World 73 Dale Street, Liverpool L2 2HT Tel: 0151 236 3662 RS Models 69 Telegraph Road, Heswall, Wirral, CH60 0AD Tel: 0151 348 4363 World Of Motion Bus and Tram Museum, 1 Taylor Street, Birkenhead, CH41 1LJ Tel: 0151 649 0948

Norfolk Anglia Model Centre 109 High Street, Gorleston, NR31 6RE Tel: 01493 664815 Auto-Loco 10 Station Road, Sheringham, NR26 8RG Tel: 01263 821777 BJ Model Railways 116 Norfolk Street, Kings Lynn, PE30 1AP Tel: 01553 773394 Bure Valley Railway Aylesham Station, Norwich Road, Aylsham, NR11 6BW Tel: 01263 733858 GE Models Platform 2, North Norfolk Railway, Sheringham Station, Sheringham, NR26 8RA Tel: 01263 821010 Great Eastern Railway Co 199 Plumstead Road, Norwich, NR1 4AB Tel: 01603 431457 Hunstanton Models 24B High Street, Hunstanton, PE36 6BJ Tel: 01485 533324 Langleys Toymaster 12-14 Royal Arcade, Norwich NR2 1NQ, Tel: 01603 621959 Snetterton Market Model Shop Snetterton Market, Norwich, NR16 2JU Tel: 01953 887878 Starlings of Sheringham St 31-33 High Street, Sheringham, NR26 8DS Tel: 01263 822368 The Card Shop 8 Greengate, Hunstanton, PE36 6BJ Tel: 01485 534466

North Yorkshire Buffers Coffee Shop & Model Railways Back O'th'hill, Storiths, Bolton Abbey, Skipton, BD23 6HU Tel: 01756 710253 Craven Model Centre 4 Mount Pleasant High Street, Skipton, BD23 1OK Tel: 01756 249170 ESRT Co Ltd Embsay Station, Skipton BD23 6QX Tel: 01756 794727 Grovers Toymaster 216-217 High Street, Northallerton, DL7 8LW Tel: 01609 773334 Modelzone Unit 30 Victoria Centre, Harrogate, HG1 1AE Tel: 01423 701955 Models-Trains-Fantasy Games 7 Railway Street, Leyburn, DL8 5EH Tel: 01969 624686 Monk Bar Model Shop 2 Goodramgate, York, YO1 7LQ Tel: 01904 659423 Puffers Of Pickering 7a Park Street, Pickering, YO18 7AJ Tel: 01751 472762 Skipton Model Centre The High Street, Skipton, BD23 1JZ Tel: 01756 797414 Starbeck Models 16 Devonshire Place, Harrogate, HG1 4AA Tel: 01423 507089 The Train Shop 41 Eastborough, Scarborough, YO11 1NH Tel: 01723 354019 York Model Railway Ltd Tea Room Square, York Railway Station, York, YO24 1AY Tel: 01904 630169

Northamptonshire Models For Sale Ltd The Barn, Low Farm, Easton Maudit, Bozeat, NN29 7NR Tel: 01933 666999 T&R Models, 20 Cannon Street, Wellingborough, NN8 4DN Tel: 01933 273388 The Model Shop, 230 Wellingborough Road, Northampton, NN1 4EJ Tel: 01604 631223 Windmill Junction, 60 Windmill Avenue, Kettering NN16 0RB Tel: 01536 522533

Northumberland Berwick Hobbies 81 Castlegate, Berwick upon Tweed, TD15 1LF Tel: 01289 308481 Cramlington Models 41 Reigate Square, Parkside Glade, Cramlington, NE23 1NW Tel: 01670 716488 The Collectors Cellar 11 Hencotes, Hexham, NE46 2EQ Tel: 01434 601392

Nottinghamshire Access Models 43-45 Castle Gate, Newark, NG24 1BE Tel: 01636 673116 Basement Models Unit 2, Hermon Street, Nottingham, NG7 1LP Tel: 0115 9705693 Bridge Street Model Shop 12 Bridge Street, Mansfield, NG18 1AN Tel: 01623 622215 Gee Dee Models 21 Heathcoat Street, Nottingham, NG1 3AF Tel: 0115 9412211 Geoffrey Allison Railways 90 Cheapside, Worksop, S80 2HY Tel: 01909 473255 MB Models 32 Conery Gardens, Whatton, NG13 9FD Tel: 01949 850063 RBS Ltd 73-75 Main Street, Long Eaton, NG10 1GW Tel: 0115 972 7152Sherwood Models, 831 Mansfield Road, Nr. Daybrook, Nottingham, NG5 3GF Tel: 0115 9266290 Modelzone 149 Upper Broadwalk, Broadmarsh Centre, Nottingham, NG1 7LQ Tel: 0115 9414892

Oxfordshire Henley Model Miniatures 24 Reading Road, Henley on Thames, RG9 1AG Tel: 01491 572684 Howes Models 12 Banbury Road, Kidlington, OX5 2BT Tel: 01865 848000 Motor Books (Oxford) 8 The Roundway, Headington, OX3 8DH Tel: 01865 766215 Osborn's Models 2-4 Marcham Road, Abingdon, OX14 1AA Tel: 01235 522700 Pendon Museum Sales Ltd 3, Poplars House, Long Whittenham, Abingdon. OX14 4QD Tel: 01865 407365 Trinders 2a-4 Broad Street, Banbury, OX16 8BN Tel: 01295 262546

Shropshire AP Models 4 Salters Court, 3 Lower Barr Newport, TF10 7BE Tel: 01952 Craven Model Trains & Railways The Purslow Bungalow Workshops, Clunbury, Craven Arms, SY7 0HJ Tel: 01588 660425 Hobby Horse 62 Whitburn Street, Bridgnorth, WV16 4QP Tel: 01746 766659 MER Industries Coreley Mill, Coreley, Ludlow, SY8 3AU Tel: 01547 520673 Sanda Games 4 Albert Place, Donnington, Telford, TF2 8AF Tel: 01952 676722 SceneryPlus 28 Scotland Street, Ellesmere, SY12 0EG Tel: 01691 624420 Shrewsbury Model Centre 32 St John's Hill, Shrewsbury, SY1 1JJ Tel: 0800 525772 or 01743 245539 The Toy Emporium 79 High Street, Bridgnorth,

WV16 4DS Tel: 01946 765134 Whitchurch Models 43 Green End, Whitchurch, SY13 1AD Tel: 01948 667766

Somerset East Somerset Models The Railway Station, Cranmore, Shepton Mallet, BA4 4QP Tel: 01749 880651 Frome Model Centre 2 Catherine Street, Frome, BA11 1DA Tel: 01373 465295 H Challis & Son 52 High Street, Shepton Mallet, BA4 5AS Tel: 01749 343527 Hendford Halt 43 West Coker Road, Yeovil, BA20 2LZ Tel: 01935 427983 Janet's Hobby 9 Fore Street, Wellington, TA21 9EU Tel: 01823 660999 JC Kingston 52 Bridge Street, Taunton, TA1 1UD Tel: 01823 275887 JJ's Toymaster 44 Regent St,Weston-Super-Mare, Somerset, BS23 1SL Tel: 01934 418151 Mainly Trains 1C South Road Workshops, Watchet, TA23 0HF Tel: 01984 634543 Minehead Toys & Models 45 The Avenue, Minehead, TA24 5BB Tel: 01643 705550 Model Masters, International House, 50a Clifton Road, Weston Super Mare, BS23 1BW Tel: 01934 629717 MRB Models 39 Locking Road, Weston Super Mare, BS23 3BZ Tel: 01934 628305 South West Digital Ltd, 1 Savernake Road, Weston Super Mare, BS22 9HQ, Tel: 01934 517303 Station Toys & Models The Station Model & Gift Shop, Bishops Lydeard, Taunton, TA4 3BX Tel: 01823 432125 Trapnells Model Shop 82 Meadow Street, Weston Super Mare, BS23 1OW Tel: 01934 620106 Wells Models & Hobbies The Old Chapel Bakery, Union Street, Wells, BA5 2PU Tel: 01749 675262 West Somerset Railway Association The Station Gift Shop, Station Road, Bishops Lydeard, Taunton, TA4 3BX Tel: 01823 432125 West Somerset Railway Plc The Buffer Stop, The Railway Station, Minehead, TA24 5BG Tel: 01643 704996

South Yorkshire Adrian White Model Railways Unit 11D, Elsecar Heritage Centre, Wath Road, Elsecar, Barnsley, S74 8HJ Tel: 01226 746907 M.G. Sharp Models 712 Attercliffe Road, Sheffield, S9 3RP Tel: 0114 2440851 Marcway Models & Hobbies 598-600 Attercliffe Road, Sheffield, S9 3QS Tel: 0114 2449170 Collectors Choice 41 The Lanes, Meadowhall Centre, Sheffield, S9 1EP Tel: 0114 2568580 Modelzone 55 High Street, Meadowhall Centre, Sheffield S9 1EN Tel: 0114 256963 Modelzone 19/21 Nether Hall Road, Doncaster, DN1 2PH Tel: 01302 367676 Rails of Sheffield 27-29 Chesterfield Road, Sheffield S8 0RL Tel: 0114 2551436 Sheffield Transport Models 206 London Road, Highfields, Sheffield, S2 4LW Tel: 0114 2553010 TAG's Massive Models 19-21 Netherhall Road, Doncaster,,DN1 2PH Tel: 0870 7005700 TAG's Massive Models 8 Fitzalan Square, Sheffield, S1 2AZ Tel: 0870 7005700 The Signalman 9 Baslow Crescent, Dodworth, Barnsley, S75 3SG Tel: 01226 246556

Staffordshire Alsager Toys & Models 58 Sandbach Road, South Alsager, Stoke on Trent, ST7 2LP Tel: 01270 882871 City Centre Models 44 Piccadilly, Hanley, Stoke on Trent, ST1 1EG Tel: 01782 274599 Hobbycraft Ventura Retail Park, Ventura Road, Tamworth, B78 3HB Tel: 01827 300800 The Old Bell 9 Lower Gungate, Tamworth, B79 7BA Tel: 01827 310320 The Train Shop 32 Bird Street, Lichfield, WS13 6PR Tel: 01543 268725 The Tutbury Jinny 9 Tutbury, Mill Mews, Lower High Street, Tutbury, DE13 9LU Tel: 01283 814777

Suffolk Bahnhof Pollards Lane, West Row, Nr Mildenhall, Bury St. Edmunds, IP28 8RA Tel: 01638 716397 Galaxy Models & Hobbies 316-318 Foxhall Road, Ipswich, IP3 8JB Tel: 01473 729279 Model Junction 10 Whiting Street, Bury St Edmunds, IP33 1NX Tel: 01284 753456 Parrs 252 London Road South, Lowestoft, NR33 0BE Tel: 01502 565695 Perfect Miniatures 86-88 Friars Street, Sudbury, CO10 2OJ Tel: 01787 375884 Scograil Model Railways 104 St Helens Street, Ipswich, IP4 2LB Tel: 01473 252009 The Train Shed Little London Hill, Debenham, Stowmarket, IP14 6PW Tel: 01728 860345

Surrey Addlestone Models 130 Station Road, Addlestone, KT15 2AR Tel: 0870 9095440 Antics 89e Woodbridge Road, Guildford, GU1 4QD Tel: 01483 539115 Dorking Model Centre 13 West Street, Dorking, RH4 1BL Tel: 01306 881747 Goldalming Central, 42 Bridge Street, Goldalming, GU7 1HL Tel: 01483 424656 Lionel Pike Garden Railway 35 Keswick Drive, Lightwater, GU18 5XE Tel: 01276 474021 Masters of Epsom 29-31 Tattenham Crescent, Tattenham Corner, Epsom, KT18 5QJ Tel: 01737 356867 Model Road and Rail 44 Central Road, Worcester Park, KT4 8HY Tel: 02083 301187 Modelzone Unit 30, The Friary Centre Guildford, GU1 4YN Tel: 01483 568682 Modelzone 30/32 Eden Street, Kingston Upon Thames, KT1 1EP Tel: 020 8549 5464 Modellers Loft 60 Croydon Road, Caterham, CR3 6QB Tel: 01883 341818 Models Of Distinction 23 The Woolmead, East Street, Farnham, GU9 7TT Tel: 01252 716981 Modern Models 10 Frimley Grove Gardens, Frimley, Camberley, GU16 7JX Tel: 01276 682313 Morningstar Hobbies 6 Bietigheim Way, Camberley, GU15 3RZ Tel: 01276 685160 Roxley Models 4 Beckley Parade, Great Bookham, Leatherhead, KT23 4RQ Tel: 01372 452976 Scale Rail Model Centre 22-24 High Street, Horley, RH6 7BB Tel: 01293 783558 The Epsom Model Shop 131 High Street, Epsom, KT19 8EF Tel: 01372 817600 Woking Models, 1 Central Buildings, Chobham Road, Woking, Surrey, GU21 1GH Tel: 01483 763023

Tyne & Wear Coats Models 44 Market Place, South Shields, NE33 1DX Tel: 0191 427 7644 Contikits Gurnard House, Main Road, Ryton, NE40 3BT Tel: 0191 4133389 Modelzone 126 Grainger Street, Newcastle Upon Tyne, NE1 5AE Tel: 0191 230 4433 Modelzone 91 The Galleria, Metro Centre, Gateshead, NE11 9YP Tel: 0191 461 0362 Rolling Stock 53 Walton Avenue, North Shields, NE29 9BS Tel: 0191 257 4328

Warwickshire Classic Train & Motor Bus 21b George Street, Royal Leamington Spa, CV31 1HA Tel: 01926 887499 Joto Hobbies 7 Lawrence Sherriff Street, Rugby, CV22 5EJ Tel: 01788 562372 Much Ado About Toys 3 Windsor Place Windsor Street, Stratford on Avon, CV37 6NL Tel: 01789 295850 Sansomes 150 Boot Hill, Grendon, Atherstone, CV9 2EW Tel: 01827 712251 Steve's Hobbies & Models 8 High Street, Studley B80 7HJ Tel: 01527 854439 The Railway & Modellers Junction 7 Leicester Street, Bedworth, CV12 8TT Tel: 024 7631 6285 Trinders 17 The Parade, Leamington Spa, Tel: 01926 470501 Wheels Model Railways Platform 5, Railway Station, Nuneaton, CV11 4BU Tel: 07966 237888

West Midlands A Oakes Ltd Oakend House, 174-180 Vicarage Road, Oldbury, Warley, B68 8JB Tel: 0121 552 1684 Ace Models 15a Fountain Arcade, Dudley, DY1 1PG Tel: 01384 257045 Die-Cast Classics 16 Chester Road, Sutton Coldfield, B73 5DA Tel: 0121 355 8862 DMB Models 7 Maple Row, Mill Street, Brierley Hill, West Midlands, DY5 2RG Tel: 01384 74744 Gaming Crypt Hobby Shop 77 Collingwood Drive, Great Barr, Birmingham, West Midlands, B43 7JW Tel: 0121 360 5080 Graingers Models & Crafts 5 Appledore Terrace, Walsall West, WS5 3DU Tel: 01922 623382 Hobbyrail 55 Riland Road, Sutton Coldfield, B75 7AN Tel: 0121 378 0680 Ian Allan Bookshop 47 Stephenson Street, Birmingham, West Midlands, B2 4DH Tel: 0121 643 2496 Midland Model Centre 18 Goodall Street, Walsall, WS1 1QL Tel: 01922 422340 Modellers Mecca 450 Albion Street, Wall Heath Kingswinford, DY6 0JP Tel: 01384 278206 Modelzone 59 Upper Mall, Merry Hill Centre, Dudley, DY5 1SR Tel: 01384 78064 Roy's Hobbies & Toys 155 New Road, Rubery, Birmingham, B45 9JW Tel: 0121 453 3280 Sleepers Models 190 Gravelly Lane, Erdington, Birmingham, B23 5SN Tel: 0121 384 3737 Southern Railways 227 Station Road, Stechford, Birmingham, B33 8BB Tel: 0121 783 5335 Tennents Trains Shop 1, 130 Hagley Road, Hayley Green, Halesowen, B63 1 DY Tel: 0121 550 1266 Trains & Hobbies 1 West Mead Centre, Winsford Avenue, Allesley Park, Coventry, CV5 9AF Tel: 02476 716059

West Sussex AABT-Collectibles 11a Culberry Nursery, Dappers Lane, Angmering, BN16 1RS Tel: 01903 774813 Langley Models 166 Three Bridges Road, Crawley, RH10 1LE Tel: 01293 516329 Mid Sussex Models 13 Junction Road, Burgess Hill, RH15 0HR Tel: 01444 232972 Model Enthusiasts Kasama, Lower Station Road, Henfield, BN5 9UG Tel: 0870 7552241 Modelzone Unit 97, County Mall, Crawley, RH10 1FD Tel: 01293 514950 Models & Hobbies 77 High Street, Steyning, BN44 3RE Tel: 01903 815732 One Way Modelsport 2 Providence Terrace, Lion Lane, Turners Hill, Crawley, RH10 4NX Tel: 01342 719190 The Engine Shed (Gaugemaster) Gaugemaster House, Ford Station Yard, Ford Road, Arundel, BN18 0BN Tel: 01903 884488 Trains, Models and Hobbies 1 Harfield Court, High Street, Bognor Regis, PO21 1EH Tel: 01243 864727 Wicor Models 9 The Precinct, West Meads, Bognor Regis, PO21 5SB Tel: 01243 837941

West Yorkshire Conways 53 Cavendish Street, Keighley, BD21 3RB Tel: 01535 604045 Frizinghall Models & Railways 202 Keighley Road, Frizinghall, Bradford, BD9 4JZ Tel: 01274 542515 Ilkley Model Centre 15 Grange Avenue, Ben Rhydding, Ilkley, LS29 8NU Tel: 01943 600964 Keighley & Worth Valley Railway Haworth Station, Haworth, Keighley, BD22 8NJ Tel: 01535 645214 Milnsbridge Models 77 Market Street Milnsbridge, Huddersfield, HD3 4HZ Tel: 01484 655276 Modelzone Unit 76 The Merrion Centre, Leeds, LS2 8NG Tel: 0113 2421070 Pennine Models 33-35 Mill Hey, Haworth, Keighley, BD22 8NE Tel: 01535 642367 Something Wicked Models 1 Wood Street, Huddersfield, HD1 1BT, Tel: 01484 537191 The Turntable11-12 Belle Vue Terrace, Blackwoodhall, Luddenden Foot, Halifax, HX2 6HG Tel: 01422 883489 Toyworld Model and Craft centre 17 Theatre Walk, The Headrow Centre, Leeds, LS1 6JE Tel: 0113 243 9800 Wakefield Model Railway Centre 260 Dewsbury Road, Wakefield, WF2 9BY Tel: 01924 374097 WBH Lord 78 Commercial Street, Brighouse, HD6 1AQ Tel: 01484 713869

Wiltshire Cheney Manor Models/Railwayania Unit 46, BSS House, Cheney Manor, Swindon, SN2 2PJ Tel: 01793 642594 Froude & Hext 83 Victoria Road, Swindon, SN1 3BB Tel: 01793 522098 Longleat Railways Longleat, Warminster, BA12 7NQ Tel: Modelmaniacs 21-23 Church Street, Calne, SN11 0HY Tel: 01249 817731 Salisbury Model Centre 37 Fisherton Street, Salisbury, Wiltshire, SP2 7SU Tel: 01722 334757 Spot-On Models & Games 49 Fleet Street, Swindon, SN1 1RE Tel: 01793 617302

Worcestershire Antics 16 St Swithins Street, Worcester, WR1 2PS Tel: 01905 22075 Handy Systems (Model Shop) 6 Vine Mews, Vine Street, Evesham, WR11 4RE Tel: 01386 422274 Kitz Models and Hobbies 5 Fish Street, Worcester, WR1 2HN Tel: 01905 610800 Model Craze 103 Lower Lickhill, Road, Stourport on Severn, DY13 8UQ Tel: 01299 877515 Steve's Hobbies & Models 34 Birmingham Road, Bromsgrove, B61 0DD Tel: 01527 880081

SCOTLAND

Aberdeenshire Models Unlimited 16 High Street, Inverarie, AB51 3XQ Tel: 01467 672277 Stevens Toymaster The Square, Ellon, Aberdeen, AB41 9JB Tel: 01358 724059

Angus Collectors Model Cars 118 Main Street Invergowie, Dundee, Angus, DD2 5BE Tel: 01382 561064 J Yule & Sons Ltd 86 High Street, Arbroath, Angus, DD11 1HL Tel: 01241 872195

Argyll & Bute Macs Model Railroading 64a Sinclair Street, Helensburgh, G84 8TP Tel: 01436 679444 William Kirkland Ltd 64/66 West Princess Street , Helensburgh, G84 8UQ Tel: 01436 674557

Ayrshire Doon Valley Models Unit 3, Carclout House, Patna, KA6 7LE Tel: 01292 531235

Fife Abbey Models Dunfermline 2 Maygate, Dunfermline, KY12 7NH Tel: 01383 731116 Parkside Dundas Millie Street, Kirkcaldy, KY1 2NL Tel: 01592 640896 Scoonie Hobbies 87 St. Clair Street, Kirkcaldy, KY1 2NW Tel: 01592 651792

Highlands Geo Durran & Son Ltd Durrans, 2 Sir John's Square, Thurso, KW14 7HN Tel: 01847 893169 The Sport & Model Shop High Street, Dingwall, IV15 9RY Tel: 01349 862346

Lanarkshire D&F Models 56 Bell Street, Merchant City, Glasgow, G1 1LQ Tel:0141 552 8044 Glasgow Model Centre 671 Cathcart Road, Glasgow, G42 8AP Tel: 0141 423 4033 Pastimes Vintage Toys 126 Maryhill Road, Glasgow, G20 7QS Tel: 0141 331 1008 Uddingston Model Centre 161 Main Street, Uddingston, Glasgow, G71 7BP Tel: 01698 813194

Lothian Harburn Hobbies 67 Elm Row, Leith Walk, Edinburgh, EH7 4AQ Tel: 0131 556 3233 Marionville Models 42 Turnhouse Road, Maybury, Edinburgh, EH12 8LX Tel: 0131 317 7010 Wonderland Models 97/101 Lothian Road, Edinburgh, EH3 9AN Tel: 0131 229 6428

Moray Moray's Models 21 Reidhaven Square, Keith, AB55 5AB Tel: 087075 66729

Renfewshire Mackay Models Studio, 56/57 Abbey Mill Centre, Seedhill, Paisley, PA1 1TJ Tel: 0141 887 9766 Paisley Model Centre 80 Arkleston Road, Paisley, PA1 3TS Tel: 0141 889 4221 814218

Sterlingshire McLaren Models 155b & 202 Grahams Road, Falkirk, FK2 7BX Tel: 01324 624102

WALES

Carmathenshire George Lewis (Toys) Market Hall, Llanelli, SA15 1YB Tel: 01554 757358

Ceredigion Albatross 29 Pier Street, Aberystwyth, SY23 2LN Tel: 01970 617836 Clocktower Models 48a Great Darkgate Street, Aberystwyth, SY23 1DY Tel: 01970 611432 Old Barn Hobbies Unit 18, Aberaeron Craft Centre, Clos Pencarreg, Aberaeron, SY46 0DX Tel: 01545 571634 Toy Museum Rhosgoch Shop, Mydroilyn, Lampeter, SA48 7RN

Clwyd Conwy Valley Railway Museum The Old Goods Yard, Betws-Y-Coed, LL24 0AL Tel: 01690 710568 Dapol Ltd Gledrid Industrial Park, Chirk, Wrexham, LL14 5DG Tel: 01691 774455 Hobby Corner 112 Chester Road, Garden Village, Wrexham, LL11 2SN Tel: 01978 355231 Model Exchange Hobby Shop 2-4 Station Road, Greenfield, Holywell, CH8 7EL Tel: 01352 713027 Rail Times 64 Abergele Road, Colwyn Bay, Clwyd, LL29 7PP Tel: 01492 530905

Glamorgan Antics 11 High Street, Cardiff, CF1 2AW Tel: 02920 229065 Bristol House Models 9 Katie Street, Blaengarw, nr Bridgend, CF32 8AB Tel: 01656 8760260 DW Models 67 Nolton Street, Bridgend CF31 3AE Tel: 01656 665435 Holt Model Railways 100 Bishopston Road, Bishopston, Swansea, SA3 3EW Tel: 01792 232264 Ian Allan Bookshop 31 Royal Arcade, Cardiff, CF10 1AE Tel: 02920 390615 Jet Models & Hobbies 27 Bartlett Street, Caerphilly, CF83 1JS Tel: 01222 880600 Kittle Hobby Banks of Kittle, PO Box 05, Ystalyfera, Swansea, SA9 1YE Tel: 01639 731005 Lendons of Cardiff 192 Fidlas Road, Llanishen, Cardiff, CF4 5LZ Tel: 029 2075 2563 Lendons of Cardiff 496/498 Cowbridge Road, East Victoria Park, Cardiff Tel: 029 2040 5559 Lord & Butler Model Railways, The Pumping Station, Penarth Road, Cardiff, CF11 8TT Tel: 02920 667225 Making Tracks 19 St. Nicholas Road, Barry, CF62 6QW Tel: 01446 722838 MIB Models 1 Lewis Buildings, Newton Nottage, Road, Newton, Porthcawl, CF36 5PE Tel: 01656 771121 Model

Tramway Shop 18 Glanffrwd Road, Glyntir, Pontadulais, Swansea, SA4 1QE Tel: 01792 885997 Risca Model Mart 1 Crescent Road, Risca, Caerphilly, NP1 6JG Tel: 01633 619697 Swansea Model Centre Unit 3, Shoppers Walk Arcade, Oxford Street, Swansea, SA1 3AY Tel: 01792 652877

Gwent Abergavenny Model Shop 1 Brecon Road, Abergavenny, NP7 5UH Tel: 01873 852566 The Railway Shop 13A Broad Street, Blaenavon, NP4 9ND Tel: 01495 792263

Gwynedd Bala Model Shop The Old Rectory, Llangar, Nr Corwen, LL21 0HW Tel: 01490 412125 Modelau Penrhyn Models Wenallt, Penrhyndeudraeth, LL48 6PW Tel: 01766 771642 Photoworld Model Railways 7A Victoria Street, Craig-Y-Don, Llandudno, LL30 1LQ Tel: 01492 871818 RA Jones & Son 35-37 High Street, Caernarfon, LL55 1RH Tel: 01286 673121 Railways Unlimited The Railway Study Centre, Tal Eithin, Isaf Llanllyfni, Caenarfon, LL54 6RT Tel: 01286 882332 Talyllyn Railway Shop Wharf Station, Tywyn, Gwynedd, LL36 9EY Tel: 01654 711012

Pembrokeshire

County Clothes 24 High Street, Haverfordwest, SA61 2DA Tel: 01437 763698

Powys Trainstop 9 Station Road, Knighton, LD7 1DT Tel: 0500 009135

JAMES MAY'S TOY STORIES

As seen on TV!

This gloriously illustrated tie-in to the popular BBC television series features exclusive imagery from all of James' toy adventures, taking a closer look at how the projects were constructed and the history of the nation's favourite toys, with illustrations and informal photography taken during filming. *Toy Stories* also offers a range of simple but fun toy-themed projects to make yourself, with step-by-step instructions and diagrams, and an extended 'anorak's corner' reference section.

9781844861071 | £20
Hardback | 272pp
245x190mm

CONWAY

Index